CHINESE
Takeaway

IN ➔ 5

KWOKLYN WAN

Publishing Director Sarah Lavelle
Assistant Editor Stacey Cleworth
Art Direction Emily Lapworth
Designer Gemma Hayden
Photographer Sam Folan
Food Stylist Katie Marshall
Props Stylist Agathe Gits
Head of Production Stephen Lang
Production Controller Nikolaus Ginelli

Published in 2021 by Quadrille
an imprint of Hardie Grant Publishing

Quadrille
52–54 Southwark Street
London SE1 1UN
quadrille.com

Cataloguing in Publication Data: a catalogue record
for this book is available from the British Library.

ISBN 9781787135789

Printed in China

CHINESE Takeaway IN → 5

KWOKLYN WAN

80 of your favourite dishes using only **five ingredients**

Photography by Sam Folan

Hardie Grant

QUADRILLE

VEGETARIAN

CONDIMENTS

DESSERTS & DRINKS

42.

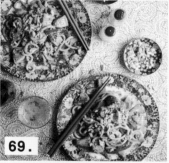

69.

81.

91.

INTRODUCTION

Raiding the store cupboard should become an international sport; it's common practice in every household around the world with busy families and singletons alike getting home from a hard day and finding there's very little to eat in their cupboards and fridges.

My *Chinese Takeaway in 5* cookbook will do away with these sorts of kitchen casualties so that in no time at all you'll be whipping up Chinese-inspired masterpieces at home with just a few simple ingredients.

Creating a delicious meal should never feel like a chore and at the end of a busy day, who really needs (or wants) to get stuck into hours of preparation and cooking, closely followed by a mountain of washing up. What better way to unwind than to lose yourself for a short time in the kitchen, safe in the knowledge that, yes, you will be eating something delicious but no, it won't take for ever to prepare and no, you don't need to do a marathon shop to get started. With just a few ingredients, you can serve up a flavoursome dinner quicker than you can place an order with your local takeaway!

As a youngster (and still now), my go-to snack is a quick bowl of 'ready in 5' ramen noodles, heartily drizzled in sweet chilli sauce – so satisfyingly moreish and no faff. Sometimes I'll pimp them up with a poached egg on top or a couple of shredded fish sticks, depending on what's lurking in the fridge at the time; sometimes I'll go soupy, other times not.

Ramen is such a versatile noodle and so quick to prepare, the little dry bricks will sit happily in your cupboard until you're ready to cook and are high on my list of recommended quick-fix options.

I urge you to experiment in the kitchen. Absolutely try every dish to the letter (I promise you won't be disappointed) but do play with the recipes too ... let every page inspire you to try combining flavours, using the following recipes as a guide and then mixing them up in your own way. Cook to your own personal taste and remember, taste is key: sample your dishes before you season and take a moment to consider what the dish needs before you go adding extra salt, pepper, sugar etc. If you're cooking with ready-made sauces, it's important to remember that they will already contain a certain amount of salt, pepper and spices and you don't want to ruin your efforts by over seasoning at the last minute. Always taste, season, and taste again!

Whether you're a straight-up carnivore, vegetarian, pescatarian or flexitarian, this book offers something for everyone. Don't ever feel confined to just one category; if you fancy Satay Chicken Udon Noodles but don't eat meat, swap out the chicken for a veggie alternative. Maybe you've been eyeing up the Baked Mushrooms with a Five Spice Crust but dinner just simply isn't dinner without a little meat; in that case use the five spice crust on a chicken breast and bake away – the world really is your oyster.

5-INGREDIENT STORE CUPBOARD

It's true that my kitchen cupboards are quite literally spilling with jars and cans of spices, sauces, dried herbs, oils and vinegars, but as a chef of many years, I'm always looking at recipe development, not to mention the simple fact that I completely lack the ability to leave my local Chinese supermarket or even the world food aisle of one of the big supermarkets carrying just the items on my shopping list! With so much variety of ingredients available in dry and preserved form, I love to keep my supplies well replenished.

Having a vast array of ingredients is not the be-all and end-all of successful cooking though, but I have assumed that you'll have plentiful supplies of just five essentials that I consider to be absolute 'must-haves' sitting in your pantry. These are salt, ground white pepper, light soy sauce, oil (vegetable, groundnut, coconut) and sugar. These basics will be listed under a separate heading, 'From the store cupboard', in each recipe so after you've stocked up on your essentials, all you'll need to consider are the main ingredients for each dish.

Quality and authenticity

As with all cooking, better results will always be achieved if you start with the best ingredients you can lay your hands on, not just from the flavour aspect but also for our own personal health benefits of eating produce and meat products that have been raised/ grown in a higher-welfare environment and not pumped full of nasties. Aim to pick up organic and free-range products where possible and consider using seasonal ingredients to make your food that much more flavoursome and nutritious, with the added bonus of being kinder on the wallet!

When shopping for specific Chinese ingredients, I would always encourage you to find and explore your local Asian supermarket. You'll find a huge variety of ingredients among the aisles, and all at reasonable prices.

Batch cooking

Whether you're looking for a spot of kitchen therapy, planning for the week/month ahead, or have simply cooked enough to feed the street, pre-making sauces and storing them in the freezer is a great way to keep your 'fresh' ingredients readily available for a quick grab-and-go meal. I like to gather the ingredients for a selection of sauces and then lock myself away in the kitchen with my favourite playlist as I chop, bubble and boil, before allowing the sauces to cool and then decanting into ice-cube trays for freezing. Once frozen, the cubes can be transferred to ziplock freezer bags and stored for up to 3 months – not that they'll last that long! Oh, and don't forget to label your bags ...

Condiments

I have included recipes for you to have a go at making your own sauces from scratch, as it really is hard to beat that totally fresh taste. But sometimes, when time is of the essence or you just don't want the faff, a generous dollop of a shop-bought marinade or sauce can be like a gift from the gods! You can buy all of the marinades and sauces that you'll need to create each of the dishes in this book but, please remember, different spice mixes will be used by each different brand so flavours will vary.

Leftovers

Taste Not Waste, people! So, you made too much filling for your Char Siu Puffs? Stuff it into that leftover tortilla wrap with a handful of salad and, voilà, tomorrow's lunch is sorted! Failing that, pop it in a sealed tub in the fridge for up to 2 days or the freezer for up to 3 months, ready to haul out and cook into your next batch of egg-fried rice. Not all dishes will lend themselves to freezing but most (shellfish excluded) will be happy to sit in an airtight container in your fridge for a day, ready for second helpings. Please do make sure that everything is thoroughly reheated before eating.

Bulking up the recipes

I've planned most of the recipes in this book to feed 2 or 4 people so it's fairly straightforward to scale up or down; however, if you're doubling up on a recipe to feed more, always check your seasoning as twice the original quantity of salt will often be too much. When cooking larger portions using a wok, you may need to cook a smaller batch, then transfer to a serving plate while you cook up the next batch, as overloading the wok will cause the ingredients to sweat and you'll lose that stir-fried flavour you get from cooking over a high heat.

EQUIPMENT AND TECHNIQUES

I will admit that many kitchen gadgets can look fancy and fun to use – until you have to wash them, and their many fiddly parts! Aside from the basics in my kitchen – saucepans, sieves, mixing bowls, wooden spoons and roasting trays – five personal equipment essentials are: my folded, Damascus steel chopper, butcher's block chopping board, seasoned wok, Chinese ladle and bamboo steamers. These serve all my peeling, smashing, chopping, frying, steaming and boiling needs. If you don't have a wok, a deep-sided frying pan will work just as well and if the thought of a chopper makes you nervous, a sharp kitchen knife will work.

CHINESE COOKING TECHNIQUES

Stir-frying

This is by far the most common method of cooking when using a wok. The wok was designed to sit above an open fire in a clay hole and the thin base and sides are designed to evenly distribute the heat throughout the entire cooking surface. You must remember that once you begin cooking you'll have to pay full attention to what is going on in the wok as you can easily burn the ingredients if you get distracted. With this in mind it is important that all of your ingredients are prepared before you begin to cook.

Steaming

This traditional Chinese cooking method is considered to be a healthy option as it requires little to no oil. Food is often cooked within a bamboo basket, and the moist heat enhances the food's natural flavours and locks in nutrients.

Deep-frying

As long as your oil is super-hot this technique of cooking not only locks in the food's flavour and nutrients, it adds a depth of texture that many other cooking methods cannot achieve. Many believe it's an unhealthy option but if cooked correctly the hot oil seals the outside of the ingredients, preventing excess oil from being absorbed, and the high heat cooks the food super-fast.

Braising

Slow-cooking in China has been perfected over thousands of years. There are many villages that are famous for their braising methods: cutting the ingredients into small pieces and braising them in small amounts of liquid. Braising makes the toughest of meats tender and juicy, where food literally melts in the mouth and slides off the bone.

Sautéing

This method uses less oil than deep-frying and a lower temperature. Meat is often cut into thin slices and coated in a cornflour batter, cooked on one side and then flipped over to be cooked on the other side. Food becomes crisp on the outside and tender in the middle.

Tenderising

You've probably noticed that when you eat at a Chinese restaurant or takeaway, the meat always seems to be supremely tender and juicy and some meats even have a silky smooth texture. The process that can create this texture is called tenderisation; the Chinese call it 'velveting'. It's a very simple process, though it does take some planning ahead, as ideally you want the meat tenderising for at least 2 hours before you cook it. Here's how I would tenderise meat or fish:

1. 1 tbsp Chinese rice wine (or use water)
2. 1 tbsp cornflour (cornstarch)
3. 1 tbsp dark soy sauce
4. 1 tbsp light soy sauce
5. 1 tsp bicarbonate of soda (baking soda)

Add all the ingredients to a large bowl along with 350–600g (12–21oz) of your sliced meat or fish. Mix everything together vigorously with your hands for 30–45 seconds; there should be no liquid left sitting in the bottom of the bowl. Cover and set aside for, ideally, 2 hours before cooking.

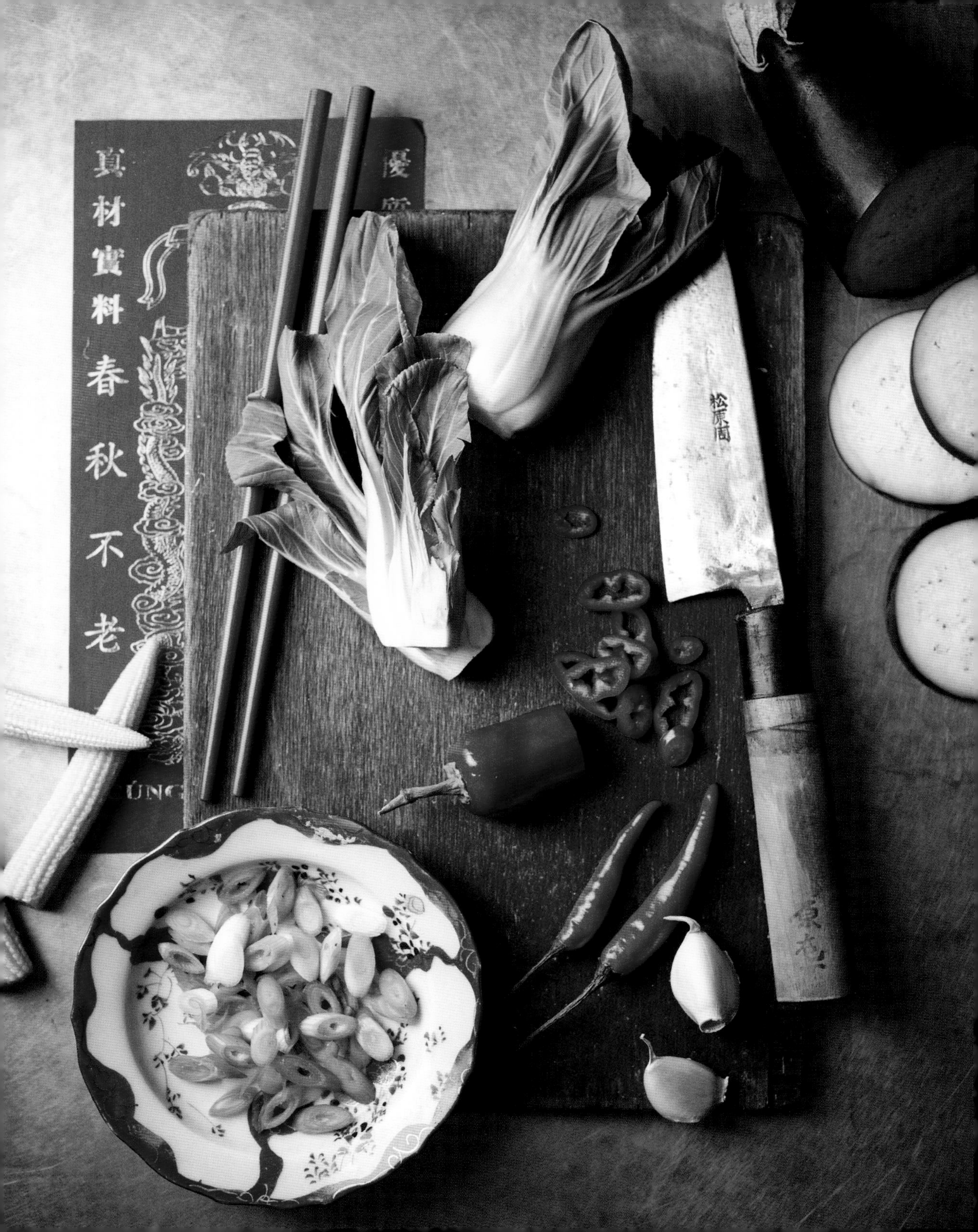
真材實料春秋不老

SOUPS

EGG DROP SOUP

This soup, so called for the method used to cook the eggs, hits all the right notes: warm, comforting, savoury and yet it still has a deliciously subtle sweetness. Found in many Chinese restaurants, it's also particularly popular in Chinese takeaways across the world.

5 MINUTES   **10 MINUTES**   **SERVES 2–4**

1 800ml (3½ cups) vegetable stock

2 1 x 420g (15oz) can creamed corn

3 2 tbsp cornflour (cornstarch) mixed with 4 tbsp water

4 2 eggs, beaten

5 1–2 tsp sesame oil

From the store cupboard
white pepper, to taste
½ tsp salt

Pour the vegetable stock into a medium saucepan and bring to the boil. Next add the creamed corn and return to the boil, before reducing to a gentle simmer and seasoning with white pepper and salt to taste.

Stir the cornflour mixture and then gradually add to the simmering soup, stirring constantly until you have reached the desired consistency. Turn the heat down to low and slowly pour in the beaten eggs, swirling and stirring the soup at the same time. Switch off the heat. Transfer the soup to serving bowls, add a drizzle of sesame oil and serve.

MUSHROOM NOODLE SOUP

Slurpy noodles, earthy mushrooms and a hot, flavoursome broth: this has been a staple food in China since the Han Dynasty of 206 BC and is still much loved today by carnivores and veggies alike.

 5 MINUTES   **10 MINUTES**   **SERVES 2–4**

1 300g (10oz) medium noodles (you can use egg or rice noodles)

2 1 litre (4 cups) chicken stock (or use vegetable stock)

3 200g (3½ cups) button mushrooms, thinly sliced

4 3 tbsp Stir-Fry Sauce (page 136 or use shop-bought)

5 3 spring onions (scallions), sliced into rings

From the store cupboard
2 tsp sugar
¼ tsp white pepper
salt, to taste

Place the dried noodle nests into a large bowl and cover with boiling water; allow to soak for 3 minutes, drain and set to one side.

Pour the stock into a medium saucepan and bring to the boil. Next add the mushrooms along with the Stir-Fry Sauce, sugar and white pepper. Bring back to the boil and then turn down to a low simmer for 1 minute. Check the seasoning and add salt and a bit more white pepper, if needed.

Divide the noodles between 2 bowls (4 if this is a starter), pour over the soup and finally sprinkle with the spring onions.

CHICKEN CURRY SOUP

Whether you like to 'bring the heat' or just linger on the cusp of spiciness, you can tailor this soup to your own palate simply by choosing whichever curry sauce mix you prefer. Deliciously warming and so quick to make, this super-light soup is a midweek supper must-try!

5 MINUTES   **10 MINUTES**   **SERVES 2-4**

1 1 litre (4 cups) chicken stock

2 1 chicken breast, finely diced

3 2 squares of Chinese or Japanese curry sauce mix (bought in a block)

4 100g (2 cups) beansprouts

5 150g (2½ cups) button mushrooms, thinly sliced

From the store cupboard
pinch of salt
pinch of white pepper

Pour the chicken stock into a medium saucepan and bring to the boil over a medium-high heat. Add the diced chicken and bring back to the boil, then turn down to simmer for 3 minutes.

Break the curry sauce mix squares into the stock and mix well, ensuring they are completely dissolved. Add the beansprouts and mushrooms, then bring the soup back to the boil before reducing to a gentle simmer for a couple more minutes. Check the seasoning and adjust to taste with salt and pepper. Serve and enjoy.

TOFU MISO SOUP

Not only is this soup utterly delicious, it also packs a punch in the nutrition arena. A great source of protein and rich in a variety of nutrients and beneficial plant compounds, you can slurp away, comfortable in the knowledge that your body will be enjoying the benefits long after your taste buds have stopped singing!

5 MINUTES   **7 MINUTES**   **SERVES 2–4**

1 1 litre (4 cups) vegetable stock

2 3 nori sheets, cut into 3cm (1¼in) squares

3 3 spring onions (scallions), sliced into rings

4 3 tbsp miso paste

5 200g (7oz) silken tofu, cut into 2cm (¾in) cubes

Place a large saucepan over a medium-high heat, add the stock and the nori sheets and bring to the boil.

Add three-quarters of the chopped spring onions and the miso paste and simmer for 5 minutes, adding the silken tofu for the last minute. Transfer to serving bowls and garnish with the remaining spring onions.

TOM YUM SOUP

Very yum and not invented by a chap named Tom.

Tom Yum soup is a type of hot and sour seafood soup originating in Thailand. Tom refers to the boiling process while yum (or yam) refers to a Thai spicy and sour salad. Sumptuously rich and heartily filling and a definite favourite of mine.

5 MINUTES   **10 MINUTES**   **SERVES 2–4**

1 1 x 400ml (14fl oz) can coconut milk

2 6 tbsp tom yum paste

3 1 courgette (zucchini), ends trimmed, halved lengthways and then cut into thin half-moons

4 175g (3½ cups) beansprouts

5 270g (9oz) cooked mixed seafood (defrosted if frozen)

From the store cupboard
pinch of salt
pinch of white pepper

Pour the coconut milk into a medium saucepan, fill the empty can with water and add that too. Stir in the tom yum paste and bring to the boil, then add the courgette and beansprouts, allowing to simmer for 3 minutes.

Add the cooked seafood and bring back up to the boil. Remove from the heat and check the seasoning, adjusting to taste if required with a little salt and white pepper. Serve and enjoy.

LIGHT
BITES

CHAR SIU PUFFS

These moreish little morsels of succulently aromatic Chinese roast pork wrapped in puff pastry will be calling to you from the cooling rack. A word of caution however: hard as it may seem (and trust me, it's hard!) you should resist the overwhelming temptation to dive straight in, as their moist, rich centres will be like molten lava straight from the oven!

2 HOURS 40 MINUTES   **3½ HOURS**   **MAKES 12–15 PUFFS**

1 1kg (2lb 4oz) pork shoulder

2 500ml (2 cups) Chinese Barbecue Sauce (see recipe 135 or use shop-bought)

3 2 star anise

4 375g (13oz) ready-rolled puff pastry

5 1 egg, beaten with 1 tbsp water

Tip
There will be leftover pork, which can stored, covered, in the fridge for 1 week; perfect for fried rice, chow mein or simply sliced and served over plain rice with some soy sauce.

Cut the pork into 2 equal pieces and place on to a large baking tray along with the Chinese Barbecue Sauce and star anise, massaging the sauce into the meat. Cover and leave to marinate for at least 2 hours or overnight in the fridge.

Remove the pork from the fridge at least 1–2 hours before you roast.

Preheat the oven to 200°C (400°F).

Uncover the pork, add 375ml (1½ cups) water and mix into the marinade that will have pooled in the tray. Place on the middle shelf of the oven to roast for 25 minutes, then turn the pork over and baste with the marinade – if it is looking a bit dry you can add more water to loosen it. Return to the oven for a further 20 minutes and repeat, returning to the oven for a final 10 minutes. The pork should be cooked all the way through and have a nice caramelised crust, which adds colour, flavour and texture. Set to one side and allow the meat to rest for 20 minutes, ensuring you reserve some of the marinade at the bottom of the baking tray. Discard the star anise.

Once the pork has rested, cut 250g (9oz) of the pork into 5mm (¼in) cubes. Put into a bowl, adding 3 tablespoons of the reserved marinade, and mix well.

Preheat the oven again to 200°C (400°F). Unroll the pastry, leaving it on the paper it was rolled up in, and use a round cutter (about 8cm/3in in diameter) to cut out pastry circles. Place 1–2 tablespoons of the pork filling into the centre of each circle and carefully pull up the sides, pinching the pastry at the top to seal in the filling. Repeat until all of the pastry has been used.

Place your puffs on to a baking sheet and brush each puff with the egg-and-water wash. Place into the oven and bake for 15 minutes. Can be served hot or cold.

PANCAKE ROLLS

Chinese pancake rolls are very popular in Chinese fish and chip shops, takeaways and restaurants. Eaten alone or dipped in your favourite sauce, these large cylindrical parcels are packed full of beansprouts and ooze as you bite into them.

30 MINUTES　　　**25 MINUTES**　　　**SERVES 4-6**

1 300g (6 cups) beansprouts

2 6 baby corn, quartered lengthways

3 30g (¼ cup) bamboo shoots, roughly chopped

4 1 cup shredded char siu pork (see Char Siu Puffs, page 24)

5 8 x 22cm (8½in) spring roll wrappers, defrosted

From the store cupboard
oil for frying
3 tbsp light soy sauce
1 tsp salt
½ tsp white pepper
2 tsp sugar

Tip
If you're making ahead, the unfried rolls can be frozen for up to a month in a sealed container. Uneaten fried rolls can also be stored in a sealed container in the fridge for up to 3 days and enjoyed as a cold snack. The cooked rolls may lose some of their crispness in the fridge but can be refreshed with a second flash in the wok or baked in the oven on a wire rack; however, please make sure the contents are fully reheated before eating if using either method.

Place a wok over a high heat until hot. Add 1 tablespoon of oil along with your beansprouts and stir-fry for 1 minute before adding the baby corn and bamboo shoots. Stir-fry for a further 1 minute and then add the shredded pork, soy sauce, salt, pepper and sugar. Continue to stir-fry for a few more minutes until everything is well combined and cooked all the way through. Place a colander over a large bowl and tip the mixture in to cool and drain.

Once the mixture has fully cooled, place a spring roll wrapper on a board with one corner pointing towards you and brush the edges with water. Spoon 2–3 generous tablespoons of mixture into the centre of the wrapper. Fold the bottom corner up over the filling, fold the side corners in to enclose the filling and create a large fat sausage shape, and then roll towards the final corner. Use a little more water to help seal the wrapper. Repeat with the remaining wrappers and filling.

Pour enough oil into a deep-sided wok so that once the pancake rolls are added they can float. Heat the oil to 170°C (340°F) and cook the spring rolls two at a time for 7–9 minutes, or until golden brown. Remove the rolls from the oil and place on a wire rack or a plate lined with kitchen paper. Once all of the pancake rolls are cooked, serve hot.

HONEY GLAZED
CHILLI WINGS

Sweet and spicy, sticky and juicy; it is going to get messy but what's not to love about these wings. Forget the popcorn, these are the perfect 'movie night in' nibbles!

2 HOURS   **50 MINUTES**   **SERVES 4**

1 500g (1lb 2oz) chicken wings
2 8 tbsp sweet chilli sauce
3 4 tbsp runny honey
4 1 tbsp dark soy sauce
5 ¼ cup toasted sesame seeds

From the store cupboard
2 tbsp light soy sauce
2 tbsp oil

Put all of the ingredients except the toasted sesame seeds into a large bowl. Use your hands to massage the marinade into the chicken, making sure everything is well coated. Cover and place in the fridge for 2 hours.

Preheat the oven to 170°C (340°F).

Toss the chicken again in the marinade before tipping the wings and sauce on to a baking tray. Bake in the oven for 20 minutes, then flip the wings over and baste in the marinade. Cook for a further 20 minutes, flip again and baste one last time. Increase the oven temperature to 200°C (400°F), then return the tray to the oven for a final 10 minutes.

Once the marinade has achieved its sticky caramelisation, remove the wings from the oven, transfer to a serving plate, sprinkle with the toasted sesame seeds and serve piping hot.

STEAMED SCALLOPS WITH GLASS NOODLES

These gloriously decadent, tender scallops sit on a nest of glass noodles and are oozing with an aromatic steaming liquor that simply must be drunk from the shell.

10 MINUTES   **5 MINUTES**   **SERVES 2-4**

1 2 nests of mung bean glass noodles

2 8 fresh scallops in their shells

3 2 garlic cloves, finely chopped or grated

4 3cm (1¼in) piece of fresh ginger, cut into thin matchsticks

5 light soy sauce or Hot Chilli Dragon Sauce (page 133)

Put the noodle nests into a large bowl and pour over enough boiling water to cover; allow to soak for 5 minutes. Drain and set to one side.

Preheat your steamer. If using a bamboo steamer, fill a saucepan with water, bring to a rolling boil and set the steamer over the pan.

Open the scallops and remove from the shells (you can ask your fishmonger to do this for you), keeping the shells for cooking and serving on. Wash the scallops and shells in cold water, then place each shell on a steady work surface. Add a fork twirl of glass noodles and lay a scallop on top. Season each with a tiny pinch of garlic and 2–3 ginger matchsticks. Once all of the scallops are prepared, carefully place them on their shells into the steamer and steam for 3–5 minutes, depending on the size of your scallops.

Transfer the scallops in their shells to serving plates and season with 1 teaspoon of soy sauce or chilli dragon sauce. Serve hot.

CRISPY WONTONS

You really can't beat the taste and texture sensation of these wontons with their savoury pork and prawn filling inside a crispy outer shell. Make time to enjoy the assembly and I promise the end result will be totally worth it!

1 HOUR 40 MINUTES   **15 MINUTES**   **SERVES 6**

1. 225g (8oz) raw king prawns (jumbo shrimp), peeled and deveined
2. 100g (½ cup) minced (ground) pork
3. 1 bunch of spring onions (scallions), sliced into thin rings
4. 30g (¼ cup) water chestnuts, finely diced
5. 1 packet of wonton wrappers

From the store cupboard
2 tsp soy sauce
¼ tsp white pepper
½ tsp salt
1 tsp sugar
vegetable oil

Dice the peeled prawns but not too finely – you still want some chunks.

Put the diced prawns, minced pork, chopped spring onions, water chestnuts, soy sauce, pepper, salt, sugar and 1 tablespoon of oil into a large bowl. Mix really well to combine all of the ingredients. Place uncovered in the fridge for at least 1 hour.

Angle a wonton wrapper on your hand so that it faces you like a diamond. With your fingertips or a spoon, spread a thin layer of water along the top two edges of the wrapper. Place 1 teaspoon of filling into the centre of the wrapper. Fold the bottom corner to the top corner to form a triangle and pinch along the edges, sealing the wanton and squeezing out the air to securely enclose the filling. Then fold and pinch the two side corners together, brushing with a little more water to help them stick together. Repeat until all of the filling has been used.

Place a deep-sided wok or saucepan over a medium heat and add enough oil so that once the wontons are added they can float. Once the oil reaches 170°C (340°F), carefully lower the wontons into the oil in batches of 5. Cook for 4–5 minutes, turning regularly to ensure even cooking and browning. Once cooked, drain the wontons over a wire rack while you cook the rest. Arrange on a plate and serve with your favourite dipping sauce.

SWEET HONEY SOY CHICKEN THIGHS

Cooked on the bone to keep them juicy and wrapped in their own crispy skins for extra flavour, these sweet, umami-rich chicken pieces will have everyone reaching for more. Napkins are recommended!

2 HOURS 10 MINUTES   **50 MINUTES**   **SERVES 4**

1 500g (1lb 2oz) chicken thighs or drumsticks (skin on)

2 5 tbsp honey

3 2 tbsp dark soy sauce

4 2 tbsp oyster sauce

From the store cupboard
4 tbsp light soy sauce
2 tbsp oil

Put all of the ingredients into a large bowl. Massage the marinade into the chicken, then cover and set to one side for 2 hours or overnight in the fridge.

If marinating overnight, remove the chicken from the fridge at least 2 hours before cooking.

Preheat the oven to 180°C (350°F).

Toss the chicken again in the marinade before tipping the pieces and marinade on to a baking tray. Bake in the oven for 20 minutes, then flip the pieces over and baste in the marinade. Cook for a further 20 minutes, flip again and baste one last time. Increase the oven temperature to 200°C (400°F), then return the tray to the oven for a final 10 minutes of caramelisation. Serve piping hot.

CHICKEN DUMPLINGS

More than just tasty parcels, dumplings represent abundance and wealth and are eaten throughout the Chinese New Year as a symbol of good luck. Whole families get together to make these yummy pouches, which can be filled with meat, vegetables and seafood.

1 HOUR 30 MINUTES   **1 HOUR**   **SERVES 6–8**

1 280g (2¼ cups) plain (all-purpose) flour

2 250g (generous 1 cup) minced (ground) chicken

3 200g (scant 1 cup) minced (ground) pork shoulder (needs to be quite fatty)

4 1 bunch of spring onions (scallions), sliced into rings

5 3 tbsp oyster sauce

From the store cupboard
¼ tsp salt
¼ tsp white pepper
1 tbsp soy sauce
1 tsp sugar
4 tbsp oil

To make the dumpling wrappers, put the flour into a bowl and gradually pour in 180ml (¾ cup) just-boiled water in a steady stream, stirring with a wooden spoon until all of the flour is damp. Pull the mixture together with one hand and form it into a ball; the dough will still be fairly lumpy at this stage.

Tip the ball out on to a smooth unfloured surface and knead with the heel of your hand for about 2 minutes until the dough is silky and slightly elastic.

Put the dough into a ziplock bag and squeeze the air out before sealing. Leave for at least 15 minutes at room temperature (or up to 2 hours), while you prepare the filling. The dough will create condensation in the bag and will feel soft when it is ready.

Mix the remaining ingredients together in a large bowl, reserving 2 tablespoons of the oil for frying. Mix well as you want an even distribution of ingredients.

Divide the dough into 32 equal pieces using a sharp knife. Taking one piece at a time, roll into a ball before flattening with the heel of your hand. Take a lightly floured rolling pin (to prevent sticking) and roll the dough until very thin but not too fragile to handle.

Place a teaspoon of filling into the centre of the wrapper, then fold one edge over to meet the other side and gently press the edges together, making sure that no filling escapes or is caught in the edge. Gather the sealed side of the parcel to form ripples around the edge of the dumpling. Place on a sheet of greaseproof paper until you are ready to cook.

Heat the reserved 2 tablespoons of oil in a flat-bottomed wok, or frying pan with a lid, over a medium-high heat. Fry the dumplings in batches of 8–10 to avoid overcrowding; fry on one side only for 2 minutes. Add 1cm (½in) water, reduce the heat to medium-low and cover with the lid, allowing the dumplings to steam until the water has evaporated. Remove the lid, increase the heat to medium-high and fry until all the bottoms are golden brown and crispy. Drain on kitchen paper and enjoy hot.

PRAWN TOASTS

I'm not exactly sure who invented this recipe but what a genius! Juicy minced prawns spread over a slice of bread, smothered in nutty sesame seeds and then deep-fried. The inspiration of a food god for sure!

15 MINUTES   **10 MINUTES**   **SERVES 6**

1 280g (10oz) raw king prawns (jumbo shrimp), peeled and deveined

2 1 egg

3 1 tbsp cornflour (cornstarch)

4 8 slices of white bread

5 70g (½ cup) sesame seeds

From the store cupboard
½ tsp salt
500ml (2 cups) vegetable oil

Put the prawns, egg, cornflour and salt into a blender and blitz into a paste.

Divide the paste into 8 equal portions and spread on to each slice of bread. Place the sesame seeds on to a large plate and press each piece of toast face down into the seeds, then knock off any excess.

Heat the oil in a deep saucepan to 180°C (350°F). Fry the bread slices one or two at a time for 2 minutes on each side, flipping occasionally to get an even colour. Drain on a wire rack or a plate lined with kitchen paper. Cut each slice into 4 triangles and serve.

KING PRAWN BEAN CURD ROLLS

These parcels deliver on so many levels; the outside is crispy and oh so light, as the bean curd wrapper gently dissolves with each bite. Then you reach the juicy king prawn filling which fills your mouth with its unique Cantonese flavours, highlighted by the fresh crunch of water chestnuts.

45 MINUTES   **15 MINUTES**   **SERVES 2–4**

1 1 x 200g (7oz) packet of bean curd sheets

2 340g (12oz) raw king prawns (jumbo shrimp)

3 5 spring onions (scallions), cut into thin rings

4 1 x 227g (8oz) can water chestnuts, drained and finely diced

5 1 egg, beaten

From the store cupboard
¼ tsp salt
pinch of white pepper
¼ tsp sugar
1 tbsp light soy sauce
4 tbsp vegetable oil

Carefully unfold the bean curd sheets and soak in warm water until they become pliable. Drain and set to one side.

Pat the king prawns dry on kitchen paper and roughly mince (grind) them (or use a blender if you have one but only use the pulse setting, as you want to retain some texture and not make a paste). Add to a bowl with the spring onions, water chestnuts, salt, pepper, sugar, soy sauce and egg. Mix well so all of the ingredients are completely combined, then place in the fridge for 20 minutes so the mixture can firm up.

Cut the bean curd sheets into 15cm (6in) squares and spoon 2–3 generous tablespoons of mixture into the centre of each wrapper; you should have around 16 squares. Take one sheet and fold the bottom corner over the filling, then fold in the side corners to enclose the filling and create a large sausage shape. Finally roll towards the top corner to seal the wrapper. Repeat with the remaining sheets.

Place a large flat frying pan over a medium-high heat and add the oil. Once the oil has heated, add the bean curd rolls in batches of 3 and cook for 2–3 minutes on each side, turning frequently to prevent sticking and to ensure the filling is completely cooked and the bean curd wrappers are crispy. Drain on a wire rack or a plate lined with kitchen paper and repeat until all of your rolls are cooked.

Enjoy warm.

BREAKFAST BAO SANDWICH

Who doesn't love a very British fried breakfast sandwich? Being a huge fan myself, I thought how could I make this more Chinese and serve it in my Hong Kong-style café bar? The answer was quite simple: let's take the classic fry-up ingredients and serve them in a freshly steamed Chinese bun.

5 MINUTES   **15 MINUTES**   **SERVES 2**

❶ 2 large mushrooms (flat or portobello)

❷ 2 pre-cooked frozen sandwich bao

❸ 4 bacon medallions or rashers (slices) of back bacon

❹ 2 eggs

❺ 4 processed cheese slices

From the store cupboard
2 tbsp oil (vegetable, groundnut or coconut), plus extra for rubbing
pinch of salt
pinch of white pepper

Clean the mushrooms and remove the stalks, then gently rub with a little oil and season with salt and pepper. Set to one side.

Preheat your steamer. If using a bamboo steamer, fill a saucepan with water, bring to a rolling boil and set the steamer over the pan. Once boiling, steam your sandwich bao for 10 minutes.

Place a large non-stick frying pan over a medium-high heat, add a tablespoon of the oil and then your mushrooms. Fry for 3–4 minutes and then flip them over and fry for a further 2 minutes. Now add the bacon and continue to fry for 4–5 minutes, flipping occasionally to prevent catching. Transfer the cooked mushrooms and bacon to a warmed plate.

Wipe the frying pan clean and heat the remaining tablespoon of oil. Fry the eggs for 2 minutes, then flip over and fry for a further minute (longer if you like your eggs well done).

Remove the sandwich bao from the steamer, place on a warmed plate and begin to build your sandwich. Layer a slice of cheese followed by the mushroom and then 2 slices of the bacon, topping with the fried egg and a final slice of cheese.

Serve and enjoy.

CHINESE BEER-BATTERED TEMPURA OYSTERS

Oysters, which were once plentiful and cheap, are now considered a luxury food – a delicacy even – and some would say, 'sophisticated'. Many shudder at the thought of eating these raw and I personally don't blame them. But lightly battered, deep-fried and served with a tasty dip, these work for me every time.

15 MINUTES   **5 MINUTES**   **SERVES 2**

1 12 raw oysters in their shells (see tip below)

2 200ml (¾ cup) Chinese rice beer, chilled

3 85g (⅔ cup) plain (all-purpose) flour, plus a little extra for dusting

4 1 lemon, cut into wedges

5 Wasabi Mayo (page 132) or your favourite dipping sauce

From the store cupboard
½ tsp salt
½ tsp sugar
oil for deep-frying

Tip
Ask your local fishmonger to shuck your oysters for you, but remember to ask for the shells.

If shucking at home, this can be done using a sharp knife or, for safety, a teaspoon handle, holding the oyster in a tea towel as the shells can be sharp.

Remove the oysters from their shells and individually pat dry with kitchen paper. Wash and dry the empty shells and place both to one side.

Pour the beer into a large bowl, sift in the flour and carefully stir with a pair of chopsticks. It is very important that you do not over-whisk. It is fine to have small lumps of flour in the batter. Add the salt and sugar and gently stir into the batter.

Pour enough oil into a heavy-based saucepan to come at least 8cm (3in) up the sides and heat to 180°C (350°F).

Dust the oysters in some extra flour, bang off any excess, then dip into the beer batter and allow the excess to drip off. Carefully drop the oysters, in batches of 6 (so as to not overcrowd the pan), into the hot oil and fry for 2 minutes until crispy and golden brown. Drain on a wire rack or a plate lined with kitchen paper.

Place the drained oysters back into their shells and arrange on a serving plate along with the wedges of lemon and wasabi mayo.

STICKY AROMATIC RIBS

Chinese barbecue ribs: aromatic, tender, unctuous, sticky, sweet and oh so familiar to every Cantonese takeaway around!

2 HOURS   **1 HOUR 15 MINUTES**   **SERVES 4**

1 1kg (2lb 4oz) ribs

2 3 star anise

3 2 cinnamon sticks

4 375ml (1½ cups) Chinese Barbecue Sauce (page 135 or use shop-bought)

5 4 tbsp golden (light corn) syrup

Put the ribs into a large bowl with all of the ingredients except the golden syrup. Massage into the meat, then cover and allow to marinate for at least 2 hours or overnight in the fridge.

Remove the ribs from the fridge and allow to come back up to room temperature; preheat the oven to 170°C (340°F).

Give the bowl a good toss and tip the ribs and any marinade that will have pooled in the bowl on to a large baking tray. Bake in the oven for 40 minutes, then increase the heat to 180°C (350°F), baste the ribs and return to the oven for another 10 minutes. Baste again and bake for a further 10 minutes, or until the ribs have begun to brown and even char a little. If you like your meat to literally fall off the bone, increase the first part of the cooking time to 1 hour before you start basting.

Remove the ribs from the oven and allow to rest for 15 minutes, then transfer to a serving plate and drizzle over the golden syrup.

CHINESE-STYLE BUFFALO WINGS

We've all heard of and probably tasted the American-style buffalo wing, smothered in its rich, spicy and very tangy sauce. Well, these Chinese-style wings deliver just as much mouth-watering action; they're crispy and juicy with a spicy tang thanks to the fermented chilli beans. Set your taste buds on high alert because there's going to be a lot going on with each bite.

10 MINUTES   **20–30 MINUTES**   **SERVES 4**

1 500g (1lb 2oz) chicken wings

2 50g (½ cup) cornflour (cornstarch)

3 2 tbsp chilli bean sauce

4 5 tbsp rice vinegar or apple cider vinegar

5 1½ tbsp tomato purée (paste)

From the store cupboard
750ml (3 cups) vegetable oil for deep-frying
2 tbsp light soy sauce
2 tbsp sugar

Use kitchen scissors to remove the tips from the wings and then carefully separate each wing into the drumette (the upper part of the wing that resembles a small drumstick) and the flat (the middle part of the chicken wing that connects the drumette and the tip). Pat each piece dry with kitchen paper and set to one side.

Pour the oil into a large saucepan and heat to 175°C (340°F).

Put the cornflour into a large bowl and dredge each wing, banging off the excess flour. Carefully fry the wings, in batches so as not to overcrowd the pan, for 8–10 minutes, or until the chicken is completely cooked. Drain on a wire rack or a plate lined with kitchen paper and set to one side.

Once all of the wings have been fried, place a wok over a medium heat and add the cooked wings with the chilli bean sauce, rice vinegar, tomato purée, soy sauce and sugar. Stir gently until all the pieces are well coated in the sauce, then transfer to a serving plate.

SEAFOOD

SWEET CHILLI SALMON WITH SOBA NOODLES

If you're looking for a dish that's simple to cook but delivers on taste and texture, looks stunning and will satisfy your hunger, then look no further. Here crispy, flaky salmon, juicy broccoli stems and chewy noodles are all richly drizzled in a sweet chilli sauce.

5 MINUTES   **25 MINUTES**   **SERVES 2**

1. 2 portions of soba noodles
2. 2 salmon steaks
3. 9 tbsp sweet chilli sauce
4. 200g (7oz) tenderstem broccoli
5. 2 tbsp rice vinegar

From the store cupboard
1 tbsp vegetable oil
pinch of salt
pinch of white pepper

Bring a medium saucepan filled with water to the boil; once boiling, add the soba noodles and cook for 5 minutes, then drain and set to one side, reserving the cooking liquid.

Heat the oil in a non-stick frying pan over a medium heat. Place the salmon steaks into the pan skin-side down, season with a pinch of salt and white pepper and fry for 5 minutes. Turn the salmon steaks over, season again with salt and pepper and fry the other side for 5 minutes. Turn the salmon steaks one last time and drizzle each with 2 tablespoons of the sweet chilli sauce, then fry for a further 2–3 minutes. Remove from the pan, loosely cover with foil and leave to rest.

Add 250ml (2 cups) of noodle water to the same frying pan and add the broccoli, allowing it to bubble in the noodle water for 2–3 minutes; if needed add more water. Add the remaining 5 tablespoons of sweet chilli sauce, along with the rice vinegar, and mix well. Then add the noodles and cook for 1 minute.

Remove the pan from the heat and use a pair of tongs or chopsticks to divide the noodles between 2 serving plates. Top with the broccoli and finally place a salmon fillet on to each pile of noodles. Drizzle with a little of the sauce and serve.

CRISPY SEA BASS FILLETS WITH BOK CHOY

After a long day these pan-fried sea bass fillets with freshly boiled rice, juicy veg and a sweet soy sauce are the perfect recipe to unwind with when you really don't want the fuss of cooking a complicated meal. Well balanced and delicious, it's a dish to feed the mind, body and soul.

10 MINUTES **30 MINUTES** **SERVES 2**

1 250g (9oz) freshly boiled rice (page 129)

2 2 tbsp dark soy sauce

3 2 sea bass fillets

4 200g (7oz) bok choy, quartered lengthways

From the store cupboard
3 tbsp light soy sauce
1 tbsp sugar
4 tbsp oil (vegetable, groundnut or coconut)
pinch of salt
pinch of white pepper

Follow the instructions on page 129 to cook the rice.

While the rice is steaming make the sweet soy sauce. Combine both soy sauces in a heatproof bowl along with the sugar. Heat 3 tablespoons of the oil in a small saucepan on a medium-high heat, until smoking. Carefully pour the oil over the soy sauce mixture, mixing at the same time – it will sizzle and spit! Set to one side.

Season both sides of the sea bass fillets with a sprinkle of salt and white pepper. Heat the remaining tablespoon of oil in a non-stick wok or frying pan over a medium-high heat and place the fillets, skin-side down, into the pan. Cook for 3–4 minutes, trying your best not to move the fillets, as you want to build up some caramelisation on the skin so that it becomes crispy. Flip the fillets over and cook for a further 2 minutes. Remove from the pan and set to one side to rest.

In the same pan as you cooked the fish, add the quartered bok choy and fry for 2 minutes. Add a pinch of salt and pepper and continue to fry for a further 1–2 minutes until tender.

Spoon a bed of rice on to 2 warmed plates, then carefully lay a fish fillet on top followed by the bok choy. Finally spoon over the sweet soy sauce mixture and serve.

CHILLI BEAN KING PRAWN NOODLES

Juicy king prawns are smothered in a classic Chinese fermented chilli bean paste and served with chewy noodles and crunchy beansprouts. From kitchen to bowl in less than 15 minutes! Give it a go – you won't be disappointed.

5 MINUTES   **9 MINUTES**   **SERVES 2**

① 1 bunch of spring onions (scallions)

② 2 nests of dried egg noodles

③ 340g (12oz) raw king prawns (jumbo shrimp), peeled and deveined

④ 50g (1 cup) beansprouts

⑤ 3 tbsp chilli bean sauce

From the store cupboard
2 tbsp vegetable oil

Prepare the spring onions by slicing the green ends into 5cm (2in) lengths and chopping the white parts into thin rings.

Soak the noodle nests in boiling water for 5 minutes until soft, then drain and set aside.

Heat the oil in a large non-stick frying pan or wok, add the spring onion greens and half the whites and fry for about 30 seconds until fragrant. Add the prawns and fry until pink, then add the beansprouts and continue to fry for a further 2 minutes.

Add the chilli bean sauce along with the drained noodles and stir to combine with the other ingredients. Continue to fry for a further 3 minutes.

Transfer to a warm serving plate and garnish with the remaining spring onion whites.

SINGAPORE KING PRAWN FRIED RICE

To this very day, if Mum doesn't eat rice with her main meal she doesn't feel satisfied; this recipe is one of her favourites. Over thousands of years the Chinese have invented many ways to enjoy rice and this Indo-Chinese twist is a stunner.

10 MINUTES   **12 MINUTES**   **SERVES 2**

1 12 large raw king prawns (jumbo shrimp), peeled

2 1 onion, finely diced

3 1 red (bell) pepper, finely diced

4 1 packet of pre-cooked basmati rice

5 2 tbsp curry powder (mild, medium or hot)

From the store cupboard
3 tbsp vegetable oil
1 tsp salt
½ tsp white pepper
1 tbsp soy sauce

Carefully cut a slit along the back of each prawn and remove the digestive tracts. Rinse under cold water, drain on kitchen paper and set to one side.

Place your wok over a medium-high heat; and once smoking add the oil, diced onion and red pepper and stir-fry for 2 minutes, then add the king prawns and cook for a further 2 minutes.

Add the cooked rice, breaking down any clumps using the back of your spoon or spatula and toss in the wok for 3 minutes. Next sprinkle in the curry powder, salt and pepper, continuing to toss the rice and mixing the ingredients well. Cook for a further 3–4 minutes – you should be able to hear the rice and ingredients frying; if not, turn up the heat and leave the pan alone until you can see the ingredients jumping in the pan and hear it sizzling away.

Once the rice is completely heated through, sprinkle in the soy sauce and mix well. Remove from the heat and serve.

SHELL-ON CANTONESE GARLIC KING PRAWNS

Mum and Dad bought the Panda Restaurant in the mid 80s; I was 11 years old and worked as a pot washer in the kitchen before moving on to the range and starting my training as a chef. It's strange how some memories remain so clear, like my fondness for the smell of this dish. I think it's the amazing combination of garlic and butter being cooked together that always tickled my nose and made my mouth water.

10 MINUTES   **7 MINUTES**   **SERVES 2**

1 16 large raw king prawns (jumbo shrimp), left whole and unpeeled

2 1 medium white onion, finely diced

3 5 garlic cloves, finely chopped or grated

4 1 green (bell) pepper, finely diced

5 4 tbsp salted butter

From the store cupboard
2 tbsp vegetable oil
1 tsp sugar
½ tsp salt
¼ tsp white pepper

Carefully cut a slit along the back of each prawn and remove the digestive tract. Rinse under cold water, drain and set to one side.

Place your wok over a medium-high heat. Once hot, add the oil and swirl around the pan to warm, then add the diced onion and fry for 30 seconds, followed by the garlic; continue to fry for 20 seconds. Next add the green pepper and after 30 seconds add the drained whole king prawns. Continue stir-frying for 2 minutes, by which time the prawns should have started to turn pink.

Add the butter and evenly sprinkle in the sugar, salt and pepper. Mix well and fry for a further 2–3 minutes until the prawns are cooked through. Serve and enjoy.

MIXED SEAFOOD FOO YUNG

A staple for many Chinese takeaways right across the world, Foo Yung is a popular dish ordered every night en masse. Fillings can include beansprouts, chicken, king prawns, spring onions and the not-so-humble pea. For this recipe I thought mixed seafood would be scrummy.

5 MINUTES   **5 MINUTES**   **SERVES 2**

1 1 bunch of spring onions (scallions)

2 6 eggs

3 270g (9oz) cooked mixed seafood (defrosted if frozen)

4 50g (1 cup) beansprouts

5 30g (¼ cup) frozen peas

From the store cupboard
pinch of salt
pinch of white pepper
1 tbsp vegetable oil

Prepare the spring onions by slicing the green ends into 5cm (2in) lengths and chopping the white parts into thin rings.

Whisk the eggs and season with a pinch of salt and pepper.

Heat the oil in a non-stick frying pan or wok. Once the oil begins to smoke, add the spring onion greens and half the white parts and fry until fragrant. Add the seafood, beansprouts and frozen peas, fry for 2 minutes then pour in the whisked eggs. Allow the egg to begin to set before starting to gently fold the mixture into itself; the egg should sit in clumps, rather than be a fine scramble.

Once the egg is softly set, transfer to serving plates and garnish with the remaining spring onion whites.

SWEET CHILLI KING PRAWN ROCKET SALAD

Sometimes all you want is a hassle-free meal: something that's light to eat but still punches you on the nose with masses of flavour. Texture combinations also play a massive part in how we taste and enjoy the food we are eating. This salad never fails to deliver on both! Give it a try; it's become a firm favourite in the Wan household.

10 MINUTES   **10 MINUTES**   **SERVES 2**

1 ½ nest of dried vermicelli rice noodles

2 16 large raw king prawns (jumbo shrimp), peeled

3 120ml (½ cup) sweet chilli sauce

4 1 bag of rocket (arugula) leaves

From the store cupboard
120ml (½ cup) vegetable oil, plus extra for frying

Heat the 120ml (½ cup) vegetable oil in a large wok to 180°C (350°F) over a medium-high heat. Using a pair of scissors, cut the noodle nests into 8cm (3in) strips. Once the oil has reached its temperature, carefully drop in a pinch of noodle strips, they should puff up – FAST! Drain on kitchen paper and repeat until all the noodles are cooked. Turn off the heat and allow the oil to cool.

Carefully cut a slit along the back of each prawn and remove the digestive tracts. Rinse under cold water, drain and set to one side.

Heat 2 tablespoons of oil in a wok over a medium-high heat and once smoking, add the drained king prawns and stir-fry for 2 minutes. Turn your wok down to medium and then add the sweet chilli sauce, continuing to stir-fry for another 2–3 minutes. If the mixture is looking dry, add a splash of water or another couple of tablespoons of the sweet chilli sauce, then turn off the heat.

Place the rocket leaves on to a large serving plate, scatter over the king prawns and the chilli sauce and gently toss through the leaves. Finally, scatter over your cooked crispy noodles and serve.

BARBECUE KING PRAWNS WITH UDON NOODLES

Udon noodles are quite different to the ones I grew up with in the restaurant; they're thicker and chewier, which creates a completely unique mouth-feel. Mixed with a classic Chinese barbecue sauce, crisp mangetout and juicy king prawns, this dish is simply delicious and will have you going back for seconds and maybe even thirds.

30 MINUTES　　**10 MINUTES**　　**SERVES 2**

❶ 16 large raw king prawns (jumbo shrimp), peeled

❷ 5 tbsp Chinese Barbecue Sauce (page 135 or use shop-bought)

❸ 175g (3½ cups) beansprouts

❹ 100g (3½oz) mangetout (snowpeas)

❺ 300g (10oz) straight-to-wok udon noodles

From the store cupboard
2 tbsp vegetable oil
2 tbsp light soy sauce
1 tsp sugar

Carefully cut a slit along the back of each prawn and remove the digestive tracts. Rinse under cold water, then pat dry with kitchen paper and add to a large bowl. Add 2 tablespoons of the Chinese Barbecue Sauce and massage into the king prawns. Allow to marinate for 20 minutes.

Heat a non-stick griddle pan over a medium-high heat, add 1 tablespoon of the vegetable oil and cook the prawns for 2 minutes on each side; transfer to a warmed plate.

Place a wok over a medium-high heat and add the remaining vegetable oil along with the beansprouts and mangetout. Stir-fry for 1 minute, then add the noodles and continue to stir-fry for a further 3 minutes. Add the remaining barbecue sauce, light soy sauce, sugar and 4 tablespoons water and mix well until piping hot. Serve in warmed bowls and enjoy.

CRISPY SQUID

A few years ago when my daughter was only 5 or 6 years old I cooked this dish and it was one of those times when everything went perfectly right. The batter was crispy and the squid literally melted in your mouth; Maya being a fussy pants though, would only eat chicken nuggets and not a lot else, so sneakily I gave her a piece to try (without the chilli salt) and said it was a nugget. She loved it! To her horror when she was a little older, I told her the truth.

10 MINUTES   **12 MINUTES**   **SERVES 2**

1 300g (10oz) fresh squid
2 2 tsp garlic powder
3 2 tsp hot chilli powder
4 50g (½ cup) cornflour (cornstarch)
5 2 eggs

From the store cupboard
½ tsp white pepper
3 tsp salt
750ml (3 cups) vegetable oil

Slice the squid into large bite-sized pieces and gently score the back of each piece with a criss-cross pattern. This will help the squid cook evenly and stop it from curling up too much.

In a small bowl mix the garlic powder, chilli powder, ¼ teaspoon of the white pepper and 2 teaspoons of the salt and set to one side. In a large bowl mix the cornflour with the remaining salt and white pepper. Whisk the eggs in a shallow bowl.

Heat the oil in a large wok or deep saucepan to 180°C (350°F). Coat each piece of squid with the seasoned cornflour and bang off the excess, then dip in the beaten egg and back into the cornflour. Gently lower the coated squid into the oil, in batches so as not to overcrowd the pan, and fry for around 2–3 minutes, turning once or twice to allow each piece to brown evenly. Remove the cooked squid from the oil and drain on a wire rack or a plate lined with kitchen paper.

Once all of the squid has been fried and drained, transfer to a large bowl, sprinkle over the chilli powder mixture and toss to coat. Transfer to a serving plate.

BLACK BEAN MUSSELS

These mussels take flavour and texture to a whole different level, hitting your senses from every angle. Salty, sweet, aromatic, juicy and soft.

10 MINUTES   **12 MINUTES**   **SERVES 4**

1 4 tbsp fermented Chinese black beans

2 1 onion, finely diced

3 2 garlic cloves, finely chopped or grated

4 1 green (bell) pepper, finely diced

5 500g (1lb 2oz) live fresh mussels

From the store cupboard
2 tbsp vegetable oil
½ tsp salt
¼ tsp white pepper
1 tsp sugar
2 tbsp light soy sauce

Soak the fermented black beans in 120ml (½ cup) warm water for 10 minutes, then drain through a sieve and set to one side.

Place a wok over a medium-high heat. Once smoking, add the oil and swirl around the wok, then add the onion and garlic and fry for 1 minute. Next add the green pepper and cook for a further 1 minute, then add the drained black beans, salt, pepper, sugar and soy sauce and mix well. Now add the mussels along with 4 tablespoons water, mix well again and cover with a lid to keep in the steam (use another large frying pan if your wok doesn't have a lid).

After 2 minutes shake the pan, keeping the lid on, and continue to cook for another 2 minutes. Uncover and stir well to ensure all of the ingredients are fully combined. The mussels should now be open (discard any that remain closed) and coated in the black bean sauce. Remove from the heat and serve.

SEA BASS ROLLS

Sharing plates are fast becoming one of the world's biggest food trends; not only is this dish great for sharing but it is also a fantastic conversation starter, as everyone around the table builds their very own perfect mouthful.

10 MINUTES **6 MINUTES** **SERVES 2–4**

1 300g (10oz) straight-to-wok medium noodles (you can use egg or rice noodles)

2 2 sea bass fillets

3 ¼ cucumber, deseeded and cut into 5cm (2in) batons (or you can use sweet pickled cucumber, page 137)

4 1 carrot, cut into 5cm (2in) matchsticks

5 8 x 22cm (8½in) rice paper rounds

From the store cupboard
pinch of salt
pinch of white pepper
1 tbsp oil (vegetable, groundnut or coconut)

Fill a medium saucepan with water and bring to the boil. Once boiling, add the noodles and cook for 2 minutes until loosened and soft. Drain and set to one side.

Season both sides of the sea bass fillets with a sprinkle of salt and pepper. Heat a non-stick wok or frying pan over a medium-high heat and add the oil. Once the oil is hot and smoking, place the fillets skin-side down into the pan. Cook for 3–4 minutes, trying your best not to move the fillets, as you want to build up some caramelisation on the skin so that it becomes crispy. Flip the fillets over and cook for a further 2 minutes, then remove from the pan and set to one side, skin-side up to preserve the crispiness, to rest.

Cut the fillets into strips. On a large platter if you have one, or individual smaller plates, arrange your cooked sea bass, drained noodles, cucumber and carrots in separate piles.

Take a rice paper round and moisten with a little water on both sides to soften, this will take about 30 seconds. Once the rice paper round is pliable, lay it flat on a clean plate and arrange your filling of fish (including some of the crispy skin), cucumber, noodles and carrot in a heaped line at the bottom third of the rice paper round. Fold the bottom third of the wrapper over the filling and then fold the loose side edges over into the centre, continuing to roll the tasty bundle forwards on to the rest of the wrapper until you have a tightly wrapped parcel.

Serve with your favourite dipping sauce.

CHICKEN & DUCK

CANTONESE CHICKEN THIGHS ON SPRING ONION FRIED RICE

Nothing screams Cantonese cuisine like the aromatic combination of garlic, ginger and spring onions. This recipe embraces all three flavours and when mixed with the perfect textures of crispy chicken skin wrapped around juicy thigh meat and served on top of lightly seasoned fried rice, it is in my opinion an all-singing, all-dancing mouth sensation.

1 HOUR 10 MINUTES   **50 MINUTES**   **SERVES 2**

1 1 bunch of spring onions (scallions)

2 4 skin-on chicken thighs

3 2 garlic cloves, thinly sliced

4 thumb-sized piece of ginger, peeled and cut into thin matchsticks

5 1 packet of pre-cooked basmati rice

From the store cupboard
3 tbsp vegetable oil
pinch of salt
pinch of white pepper
½ tbsp light soy sauce

Prepare the spring onions by slicing the green ends into 5cm (2in) lengths and the white parts into fine rings.

Put the chicken thighs into a large bowl with the garlic, ginger and the spring onion greens along with 2 tablespoons of the oil and a pinch of salt and pepper. Massage the mixture into the meat, then cover and leave to marinate for at least 1 hour (or leave in the fridge overnight).

Preheat the oven to 180°C (350°F). Put the marinated chicken on to a baking tray and roast for 30–40 minutes, or until cooked and the juices run clear. Remove from the oven and allow to rest.

Heat a non-stick frying pan or wok with the remaining tablespoon of oil. Once the oil begins to smoke, add half the spring onion whites and fry for about 30 seconds until fragrant. Add the rice and use the back of a wooden spoon to break up any rice clumps. Continue to fry for 3–5 minutes, seasoning with salt and pepper. Once the rice is fully heated, add the soy sauce and mix well.

Divide the rice between 2 plates, top with the cooked chicken thighs, garnish with the remaining spring onion whites and enjoy.

SATAY CHICKEN UDON NOODLES

Even I was surprised at just how quick this dish was to cook; no sooner had I started the dish, than it was on my plate and being scoffed. Washing up consisted of just my wok and the wooden spoon I used. Chewy noodles, juicy chicken, crunchy onions and peppers smothered in a rich spicy satay sauce. Lovely!

10 MINUTES   **8 MINUTES**   **SERVES 2**

1 2 chicken breasts, cut into bite-sized pieces

2 1 white onion, cut into strips

3 1 green (bell) pepper, cut into strips

4 4 tbsp satay dipping sauce (or use 2–3 tbsp satay paste, to taste)

5 300g (10oz) straight-to-wok udon noodles

From the store cupboard
2 tbsp oil (vegetable, groundnut or coconut)
1 tsp salt
pinch of white pepper

Tip
Add a sprinkle of crushed salted peanuts just before serving to add a lovely crunch.

Heat a large non-stick wok over a medium-high heat and add the oil. Add the chicken and allow to brown on one side, then stir in the onion and green pepper for 1–2 minutes to soften.

Season with the salt and pepper, then stir in the satay dipping sauce, along with 250ml (1 cup) water. Once all of the ingredients are well combined in the sauce, add the noodles and cook for 2 minutes, stirring frequently to separate the noodles. Serve immediately.

ASIAN-STYLE CRISPY DUCK SALAD

I'm really not sure that anything beats crispy duck on flavour, especially crispy duck seasoned with Chinese five spice and served with sweet, juicy orange segments, crunchy salad and hoisin sauce. The flavour and texture profile of this dish is quite simply magical.

5 MINUTES   **12 MINUTES**   **SERVES 2**

1 1 large duck breast

2 1 tsp Chinese five spice

3 2 tbsp hoisin sauce

4 1 bag of mixed salad leaves

5 1 orange, peeled and cut into 2cm (¾in) cubes (you can also use pear, mango, lychee or pomegranate)

From the store cupboard
salt
white pepper

Season the duck breast on both sides with a pinch of salt and pepper and ½ teaspoon of the Chinese five spice. Heat a dry non-stick wok over a medium-high heat, then place the breast into the hot wok, skin-side down. Turn down the heat to medium and cook for 2–3 minutes, or until the skin is golden brown, then turn the breast over and cook for a further 3–5 minutes. Remove from the pan and allow to rest for 5 minutes, then cut into thin slices.

Wipe your wok clean and reheat over a medium-high heat. Add the sliced duck and cook until crispy, seasoning again with a pinch of salt and pepper and the remaining five spice. Mix well and transfer to a plate lined with kitchen paper to drain.

In a small bowl combine the hoisin sauce with 2 tablespoons water.

Arrange your salad leaves on a large plate and top with the cooled drained duck and orange cubes. Drizzle with the hoisin dressing and toss together. Serve and enjoy.

CHICKEN CHOW MEIN

Chow mein is a firm favourite in Chinese takeaways and restaurants around the world. A top tip when cooking this dish is to *take your time.*

The word 'chow' literally means 'fried' so try not to overcrowd your wok as you want the noodles to really sizzle in the oil as they cook. This not only imparts flavour but also adds another layer of texture to the dish.

10 MINUTES   **12 MINUTES**   **SERVES 2**

1 2 nests of dried egg noodles
2 5 spring onions (scallions)
3 1 chicken breast, cut into bite-sized slices
4 175g (3½ cups) beansprouts
5 4 tbsp Stir-Fry Sauce (page 136 or use shop-bought)

From the store cupboard
3 tbsp vegetable oil
¼ tsp white pepper
½ tsp white sugar

Bring 800ml (3½ cups) water to the boil in a medium saucepan, then add the noodle nests and cook for 5 minutes until soft. Drain and set to one side.

Prepare the spring onions by cutting the green parts into 5cm (2in) pieces and then halving these lengthways. Slice the white parts into rings.

Heat your wok over a medium heat until smoking, then add the oil along with the sliced chicken and cook for 3–4 minutes. Once the chicken is nearly cooked through, add the spring onion greens and beansprouts and cook for a further minute, then add the drained noodles. Stir-fry for a further 3–5 minutes, ensuring the noodles are well combined with the rest of the ingredients and you've also allowed them time to crisp up a little. Add the pepper, sugar and Stir-Fry Sauce and continue to cook for a further 2 minutes.

Remove from the heat and transfer to 2 plates. Sprinkle with the remaining spring onion whites.

CHICKEN & MUSHROOMS ON BOILED RICE

Rich, saucy, chicken breast chunks and mushrooms served on a mound of fluffy boiled rice; this dish is comfort cooking at its simplest and best.

10 MINUTES **10 MINUTES** **SERVES 2**

1 1 onion, diced

2 1 chicken breast, cut into bite-sized slices

3 300g (5 cups) mushrooms of your choice, cut into bite-sized pieces

4 3 tbsp oyster sauce

5 250g (9oz) freshly boiled rice (page 129 or use a packet of pre-cooked rice)

From the store cupboard
2 tbsp vegetable oil
1 tbsp light soy sauce
¼ tsp salt
pinch of white pepper
1 tsp sugar

Heat a non-stick wok to smoking over a medium-high heat, then add the oil and onion. Cook for 30 seconds, then add the chicken and continue to stir-fry for 3 minutes. Next add the mushrooms and cook for 30 seconds, then turn the heat down to medium and cover with a lid for 3–4 minutes.

Remove the lid, turn the heat back up to medium-high and add the oyster sauce, soy sauce, salt, pepper and sugar. Mix well and cook for a further 1–2 minutes. Once you are happy that the chicken is cooked all the way through, serve over the steamed rice.

STICKY DUCK LEGS WITH POMEGRANATE, CASHEW NUT & MIXED LEAF SALAD

Rich duck meat smothered in a sweet plum sauce is food wizardry at its finest, delivering a taste of sweet and savoury heaven. So how can we improve on perfection? Simply add pockets of pomegranate explosions with creamy cashew nuts and crispy salad leaves.

55 MINUTES   **1 HOUR**   **SERVES 2**

1   2 duck legs

2   120ml (½ cup) plum sauce, loosened with 2 tbsp water

3   1 pomegranate

4   1 bag of mixed salad leaves

5   30g (¼ cup) cashew nuts

From the store cupboard
½ tbsp vegetable oil
pinch of salt
pinch of white pepper

Put the duck legs into a bowl with the oil, salt and pepper and massage together, then allow to marinate at room temperature for 30 minutes. Preheat the oven to 180°C (350°F).

Put the marinated duck legs into a baking tray and roast for 20 minutes. Remove from the oven and baste with the plum sauce, reserving 3–4 tablespoons of the sauce for dressing the finished dish, then reduce the oven temperature to 170°C (340°F) and return the tray to the oven. After 10 minutes turn the legs over, baste again and return to the oven for a further 10 minutes. Repeat with two more turns and bastes, allowing a sticky glaze to build up. Remove from the oven and allow to rest for 20 minutes.

Chop the pomegranate in half and holding the open side against your palm and splayed fingers over a bowl, tap the skin with a wooden spoon to release the seeds.

Once the duck has rested, carefully remove the meat from the bone, shredding it at the same time, and set to one side.

Arrange the salad leaves in a shallow bowl and add the shredded duck. Dress with the remaining plum sauce and toss to coat, finally sprinkling with the pomegranate seeds and cashew nuts. Serve immediately.

OYSTER SAUCE CHICKEN ON CRISPY NOODLES

This dish is served in the finest of Cantonese restaurants worldwide. These delectable noodles are fried until crispy and then smothered in a sumptuous, aromatic gravy with meat and vegetables.

10–15 MINUTES   **15 MINUTES**   **SERVES 2**

1 2 nests of dried thin egg noodles

2 2 chicken breasts, cut into bite-sized pieces

3 1 large white onion, thinly sliced

4 1 x 425g (15oz) can straw mushrooms, drained

5 3 tbsp oyster sauce

From the store cupboard
6 tbsp vegetable oil for shallow frying
pinch of salt
pinch of white pepper

Soak the noodle nests in boiling water for 5 minutes until soft, then drain and set aside for a further 5–10 minutes to dry.

Heat a non-stick frying pan or wok with 4 tablespoons of the oil until shimmering. Carefully add the drained noodles to form a single thin layer in the oil. Allow the noodles to fry on one side for 2–3 minutes until crispy, then carefully turn the entire layer and cook for a further 1–2 minutes, or until crispy on the other side. Remove from the pan and drain on kitchen paper before transferring to a serving plate.

Wipe out the frying pan or wok, place over a medium heat and add the remaining 2 tablespoons of oil. Once the oil begins to smoke, add the chicken pieces and fry for 3 minutes, stirring occasionally. Add the onion and continue to fry for 1–2 minutes until translucent, then add the straw mushrooms along with the oyster sauce and 4 tablespoons water. Stir to combine and allow to simmer until reduced by about half. Check and adjust the seasoning.

If you like more sauce, simply add a little more water and an additional 1–2 tablespoons of oyster sauce. Serve heaped over the crispy noodles.

SWEET SOY PULLED CHICKEN

Perfect served in a freshly steamed bao or even a freshly baked baguette, with soy-pickled cucumber and shredded lettuce; close your eyes and with a mouthful of this sweet, succulent chicken, let the flavours transport you to the bustling street markets of Hong Kong.

 5 MINUTES   **1 HOUR**   **SERVES 4**

1 2 skinless and boneless chicken breasts

2 80ml (⅓ cup) rice vinegar

3 160g (½ cup) blackberry jam

4 1 tsp celery salt

5 1 tbsp chilli flakes

From the store cupboard
120ml (½ cup) light soy sauce
50g (¼ cup) sugar

Put all the ingredients into a saucepan that has a tight-fitting lid along with 375ml (1½ cups) water. Bring to the boil and then turn down to a low simmer and place the lid firmly on.

After 45 minutes remove the lid and bring back up to the boil. Once the liquid has reduced by two-thirds, remove from the heat and allow to cool for 15 minutes.

Carefully shred the chicken, then mix with the remaining cooking liquid and serve.

CHICKEN & BROCCOLI IN STIR-FRY SAUCE

This wholesome dish is exactly the reason why you need not be so quick to reach for that takeaway menu. Having complete control of the ingredients you're using will enable you to munch away guilt-free, as you tuck into a Chinese takeaway-style dish with complete peace of mind (and a healthier pocket).

25 MINUTES   **10 MINUTES**   **SERVES 2**

1 1 large chicken breast (about 170g/6oz), cut into bite-sized slices

2 4 tbsp Stir-Fry Sauce (page 136 or use shop-bought)

3 300g (10oz) broccoli florets

4 1 garlic clove, finely chopped or grated

5 1 tbsp cornflour (cornstarch) mixed with 2 tbsp water

From the store cupboard
2 tbsp vegetable oil
1 tsp sugar

Put the chicken slices into a large bowl, add half the Stir-Fry Sauce and massage into the chicken; set to one side for 20 minutes.

While the chicken is marinating, bring a saucepan of water to the boil and blanch the broccoli florets for 2–3 minutes; drain and set to one side.

Heat a non-stick wok over a medium heat, then add the oil and garlic, frying for 30 seconds until fragrant and taking care not to burn the garlic. Add the marinated chicken slices and gently fry for 2–3 minutes until nearly cooked through. Add the blanched broccoli along with 375ml (1½ cups) water, the sugar and the remaining 2 tablespoons of Stir-Fry Sauce. Bring to the boil and then turn down to simmer for 3 minutes.

Give your cornflour mixture a good stir, then slowly drizzle it into the sauce, stirring continuously. Once the sauce has thickened, remove from the heat and serve.

ROASTED CHICKEN THIGHS IN OYSTER SAUCE

Over the centuries, the Chinese, and especially the Hakka people, have perfected the art of roasting meats. Following this tradition and the knowledge passed down to me from my dad and his father before him, my roasted chicken thighs are first caramelised in a pan with classic Cantonese flavours of ginger and spring onion, before being placed in the oven to continue cooking in a rich, aromatic gravy.

10 MINUTES   **40 MINUTES**   **SERVES 2**

❶ 3 tbsp rice wine

❷ 3 tbsp oyster sauce

❸ 4 spring onions (scallions), cut into 5cm (2in) lengths

❹ 2 tbsp grated fresh ginger

❺ 4 chicken thighs

From the store cupboard
1 tbsp vegetable oil
pinch of salt
pinch of white pepper

Stir the rice wine and oyster sauce together in a small bowl and set to one side.

Preheat the oven to 180°C (350°F).

Place a non-stick wok or frying pan over a medium-high heat. Once hot, add the oil, spring onions and ginger and fry for 45 seconds until fragrant.

Season each chicken thigh with a pinch of salt and pepper and place skin-side down into the hot pan, then turn the heat down to medium and cook for 2–3 minutes. Once the chicken skin has browned, flip it over so it can brown for a further 2–3 minutes on the other side.

Transfer to a small baking tray and pour over the oyster sauce mixture, then bake in the oven for 30 minutes, basting the chicken with the sauce halfway through the cooking time.

Serve with your favourite noodles or steamed rice and vegetables.

DRUNKEN CHICKEN SOUP

Potently aromatic and definitely one for a 'quiet night in' ... don't eat and drive, folks! Instead stay home and bask in the internal warmth of this hearty broth.

10 MINUTES   **40 MINUTES**   **SERVES 4–6**

1 400g chicken thigh fillets, skinned and boneless, if preferred

2 2 thumb-sized pieces of fresh ginger, roughly sliced

3 1.5 litres (6 cups) Chinese rice wine

4 2 tbsp brandy

5 2 tbsp pure sesame oil

From the store cupboard
3 tbsp vegetable oil
1 tsp salt, plus extra to taste
¼ tsp white pepper, plus extra to taste
1 tsp sugar

Cut the chicken into bite-sized pieces, removing any excess fat.

Heat a large saucepan or deep-sided wok over a medium-high heat, add the vegetable oil and ginger and fry for 45 seconds, or until fragrant. Add the chicken pieces and cook for 8–10 minutes until gently browned.

Pour in the Chinese rice wine and brandy and bring to the boil. Allow to boil for a couple of minutes, then add 875ml (3¾ cups) water along with the salt, white pepper and sugar. Bring back to the boil and then turn down to simmer for 30 minutes. During the cooking process you may find that a scum forms on the top of the soup; skim this off and discard it.

Once the chicken is fully cooked, have a final taste and adjust the seasoning to your liking. Drizzle with the sesame oil and serve.

SINGAPORE CHOW MEIN

Indo-Chinese flavours have become increasingly popular in the UK over the last 10 years, thanks to the explosion of street food markets in most major cities. This dish is a classic Indo-Chinese creation mixing ingredients from China with spices from India.

30 MINUTES   **12 MINUTES**   **SERVES 2**

1 2 chicken breasts or 300g (10oz) shredded char siu pork (see Char Siu Puffs, page 24)

2 1 nest of dried egg noodles

3 1 red (bell) pepper, cut into strips

4 175g (3½ cups) beansprouts

5 1 tbsp mild curry powder

From the store cupboard
3 tbsp vegetable oil
½ tsp salt
¼ tsp white pepper
½ tsp sugar

Bring 800ml (3½ cups) water to the boil in a medium saucepan. Add the chicken breasts, bring back to the boil and then reduce to a simmer and cook for 12–15 minutes. Drain and set to one side. Once the chicken has cooled, cut into thin strips.

Meanwhile bring another 800ml (3½ cups) water to the boil in another saucepan. Add the dried egg noodle nest and cook for 5 minutes until soft. Drain and set to one side.

Place a wok over a medium heat; once it begins to smoke add the vegetable oil along with the red pepper strips and cook for 1 minute, then add the beansprouts and cook for a further minute. Add the curry powder and continue to cook for a further 2 minutes. Add the salt, pepper and sugar and mix well.

Add the cooled sliced chicken (or pork, if using) and drained noodles to the wok and continue to cook for a further 5–8 minutes, making sure all of the ingredients are well combined and heated all the way through, allowing the noodles to catch some colour in the wok.

Serve and enjoy.

LEMON CHICKEN

Instantly recognisable as a Chinese takeaway classic with its thick, rich, lemony sauce over crispy chicken pieces, your guests will be forgiven for thinking you've cheated and ordered in from their favourite restaurant!

5 MINUTES   **12 MINUTES**   **SERVES 2**

1 120ml (½ cup) lemon cordial

2 1 tbsp custard powder (instant vanilla pudding mix)

3 2 chicken breasts

4 100g (1 cup) cornflour (cornstarch)

5 1 egg, beaten

From the store cupboard
3 tbsp sugar
750ml (3 cups) vegetable oil
½ tsp salt

Mix the lemon cordial, custard powder and sugar together in a small saucepan, then place over a low heat, stirring constantly to combine the ingredients. Once the sauce has thickened, turn off the heat.

Heat a large saucepan or deep-sided wok over a medium-high heat and fill no more than two-thirds with oil. The oil should be deep enough so that once the chicken is added it can float in the oil. Heat to 170°C (340°F).

Butterfly each chicken breast and season with the salt. Tip the cornflour on to a large plate and dredge the chicken, banging off any excess. Dip the coated chicken in the beaten egg and then dredge in cornflour for a second time, banging off the excess.

Carefully lower the chicken into the hot oil, cooking for 6–8 minutes, or until the chicken is golden brown, crispy and cooked all the way through. If you have a food probe thermometer, the internal temperature of the chicken should be at least 78°C (170°F). Transfer to a wire rack or a plate lined with kitchen paper to drain.

Reheat the lemon sauce while you slice the chicken. Arrange the chicken on a plate and pour over the sauce.

MARINATED CHICKEN SKEWERS

Don't limit this chicken to barbecues and picnics – these tasty skewers make a great starter dish or easy snack, eaten straight from the stick or eased away and stuffed into a fresh wrap with a mound of salad and dollop of mayo!

2 HOURS 10 MINUTES   **40 MINUTES**   **SERVES 4**

1 340g (12oz) chicken breast, cut into 3cm (1¼in) cubes

2 80ml (⅓ cup) honey

3 3 garlic cloves, finely chopped or grated

4 juice of 1 lemon

From the store cupboard
250ml (1 cup) light soy sauce

If you are using wooden or bamboo skewers, soak them in water for at least 1 hour before using.

Put all of the ingredients into a large bowl and mix well, making sure the chicken is well coated. Cover and allow to marinate for at least 2 hours.

Preheat the oven to 180°C (350°F). Thread 3 cubes of chicken on to each skewer, then place on a foil-lined baking tray. I'd recommend 2 skewers per person. Once all of the chicken has been threaded on to your skewers, spoon over the remaining marinade. Bake in the oven for 40 minutes, basting and turning the skewers every 15 minutes.

Once you are happy that the chicken is cooked through, transfer to a serving plate. These are best eaten warm but are also tasty as a cold snack or filling for baguettes, wraps or pittas.

MEAT

CHILLI & SALT PORK CHOPS

I used to love watching my dad cook this dish; he would use paper bags to help lock in all the flavour while the pork chops were deep-fried. I remember standing in the kitchen stapling the old-style paper bags together to form sealed pockets filled with the marinated pork and spices. These were then slid gently into a pan of hot oil to cook thoroughly while retaining the juicy marinade. The drained bags were then served still sealed and cut open at the table for each guest, releasing their delicious aroma and fresh pool of cooking liquor.

10 MINUTES **20 MINUTES** **SERVES 2**

❶ 2 pork chops

❷ 1 tbsp Chinese five spice

❸ 1 large white onion, finely diced

❹ 1 green (bell) pepper, finely diced

❺ 2 bird's-eye chillies, finely diced

From the store cupboard
2 tbsp vegetable oil
salt
white pepper

Heat 1 tablespoon of the oil in a large non-stick frying pan or wok over a medium heat until shimmering. Add the pork chops, seasoning with a pinch each of salt and pepper. Allow the chops to caramelise on one side for 6–8 minutes, then flip over and repeat on the other side, seasoning again with salt and pepper. Remove from the pan and set to one side to rest. Once rested, slice the chops into bite-sized slices.

Mix the five spice together in a bowl along with ½ teaspoon salt and ¼ teaspoon pepper and set to one side.

Place a non-stick frying pan or wok over a medium heat and add the remaining oil; once smoking, add the onion and green pepper. Fry for 2 minutes, then add the chillies and fry for a further minute, mixing well.

Turn off the heat, add the sliced pork to the pan along with the mixed seasoning and toss well to cover. Transfer to a plate and enjoy.

MISO STEAK ON STIR-FRIED VEGETABLES

Miso paste is a fantastic way of injecting flavour into soups and rice dishes and for marinating meats. The umami flavouring creates a smooth and silky texture in the mouth and this, mixed with the charred yet juicy pieces of steak, results in an amazing taste and texture combination.

2 HOURS 5 MINUTES **12 MINUTES** **SERVES 2**

1 3 tbsp rice wine

2 2 tbsp red miso paste

3 1 garlic clove, finely chopped or grated

4 2 x 150g (5oz) steaks (you can use fillet or sirloin)

5 1 x 320g (11oz) bag of stir-fry vegetables

From the store cupboard
3 tsp sugar
2 tbsp oil
½ tsp salt
¼ tsp white pepper
2 tbsp light soy sauce

In a large bowl mix together 2 teaspoons of the sugar, 2 tablespoons of the rice wine, the miso paste and the garlic. Add the steak and massage the marinade thoroughly into the meat. Cover and set aside for 2 hours.

Place a non-stick wok over a medium-high heat, add 1 tablespoon of the oil and fry the steaks for 3 minutes on each side for medium rare or cook a little longer if you prefer your steak well done. Transfer to a plate and allow to rest for a couple of minutes.

Add the remaining oil to the wok followed by the bag of prepared stir-fry vegetables. After 3–5 minutes, season with the salt, pepper, light soy sauce and the remaining rice wine and sugar. Mix well and stir-fry for a further 2–3 minutes, then transfer to a serving plate.

Slice your cooked steak into bite-sized slices and arrange over the top of the vegetables.

CRISPY BELLY PORK

I find that visiting a traditional Chinese restaurant is a sensory explosion; my local restaurant hangs roasted ducks perfectly in the windows alongside slabs of belly pork with its crispy skin and juicy meat. The gloriously rich colours and smells entice my family in every time.

20 MINUTES   **1 HOUR 50 MINUTES**   **SERVES 4**

① 1kg (2lb 4oz) pork belly
② 2 tbsp Chinese rice wine
③ 1½ tbsp Chinese five spice
④ 2 tbsp rice vinegar
⑤ 125g (½ cup) rock salt

From the store cupboard
2 tsp salt
1 tsp white pepper
sugar for dipping

Using a sharp skewer, ice pick, or meat tenderiser, pierce the skin of the pork, trying not to puncture the meat underneath. The more holes you can pierce into the skin the crispier it will be at the end.

Lay the pork belly skin-side down. Massage the rice wine into the meat side only, followed by the Chinese five spice, the 2 teaspoons of salt and the white pepper. Now place the pork belly into a dish skin-side up, pat dry the skin with kitchen paper and place into the fridge, uncovered, overnight.

When you are ready to cook preheat the oven to 180°C (350°F).

Place the marinated pork on to a piece of foil. Fold all four edges up the sides of the pork belly, covering the meat but not the skin. Dry the skin again with kitchen paper and then brush with the rice vinegar. Cover the skin completely in the rock salt and place it into the oven for 1 hour.

After 1 hour, remove the salt crust from the pork belly and transfer the meat to a clean baking tray, discarding the foil. Return the pork belly to the oven uncovered for 30–40 minutes. Finally sit the pork under a hot grill (broiler) for 8–10 minutes until super crispy but not burnt.

Transfer to a wire rack to cool. Once cooled, turn the pork over (skin-side down) and slice into bite-sized pieces. Arrange on a plate skin-side up and serve with a bowl of sugar to dip the pork in to.

AROMATIC LAMB CHOPS

Lamb is a popular meat in China and is prepared in many different ways; from serving in hot pots or on skewers to spiced with Sichuan peppercorns, deep-fried and roasted. My recipe for this versatile meat uses a Cantonese marinade which subtly flavours the meat.

I have such fond memories of Dad grilling lamb chops at home so, Dad, this dish is for you.

10 MINUTES   **8 MINUTES**   **SERVES 4**

1. 5 spring onions (scallions)
2. 5cm (2in) piece of fresh ginger, peeled
3. 5 garlic cloves
4. 8 lamb chops
5. 1 tsp ground black pepper

From the store cupboard
3 tbsp vegetable oil, plus a little extra for griddling
3 tbsp light soy sauce
1 tbsp sugar
1 tsp salt

Put the spring onions, ginger, garlic, vegetable oil, soy sauce and sugar into a blender and blitz into a paste.

Rub the marinade into each lamb chop; once the lamb is completely coated, cover with cling film (plastic wrap) or foil and allow to marinate for at least 2 hours or overnight in the fridge.

Preheat a griddle pan over a medium-high heat, drizzle both sides of the chops with a little oil and sprinkle with the salt and black pepper. Cook the lamb for 3–4 minutes on each side, or until cooked to your liking.

STICKY HOISIN GLAZED PORK

The Chinese learnt thousands of years ago that when you marinate meat, it not only imparts it with flavour but also tenderises it. These pork chops are marinated in an aromatic sweet sauce; once cooked they remain juicy and succulent with the unmistakable flavours of Cantonese roast meats.

1 HOUR 10 MINUTES   **16 MINUTES**   **SERVES 4**

1 6 tbsp hoisin sauce

2 2 garlic cloves, finely chopped or grated

3 4 pork chops

From the store cupboard
3 tbsp light soy sauce
1 tsp sugar
3 tbsp vegetable oil

In a small bowl, mix together the hoisin sauce, soy sauce, sugar and 5 tablespoons water and set to one side.

Preheat a saucepan over a medium heat, add 1 tablespoon of the oil and fry the garlic for 30 seconds until fragrant. Add the sauce mix and bring to the boil, then turn down to a simmer and reduce by a third. Remove from the heat and allow it to cool.

Place the pork chops into a ziplock bag, poor in the sauce mix and seal, squeezing out any excess air. Marinate for at least 1 hour.

Remove the chops from the bag. Shake off any excess marinade and reserve for later. Place a frying pan or wok over a medium-high heat, add the remaining oil and then add the chops, cooking on one side until golden brown, then flipping over and cooking until browned. Reduce the heat to medium and continue cooking for about 10 minutes until the chops are cooked all the way through. Transfer to a plate and allow to rest for 10 minutes.

While the pork is resting, wipe out any excess oil from your wok and tip in the leftover marinade along with 2 tablespoons water. Slowly bring to a simmer for 2 minutes, then remove from the heat.

Arrange the rested chops on plates and spoon over the sauce.

BRAISED BELLY PORK ON YELLOW BEAN NOODLES

Braising is a very popular technique of cooking in China. The slow cooking process makes the meat tender and any fat literally melts in the mouth. As the meat gently cooks away in the pot it takes on all of those lovely flavours you've added. Served on top of sweet aromatic noodles, this dish ticks all the boxes.

 5 MINUTES   **1 HOUR 5 MINUTES**   **SERVES 4**

1 2 tbsp dark soy sauce

2 4 tbsp yellow bean sauce

3 2 tbsp Chinese rice wine

4 350g (12oz) piece of belly pork

5 300g (10oz) straight-to-wok noodles (use your favourite)

From the store cupboard
6 tbsp light soy sauce
1½ tbsp vegetable oil
pinch of salt
pinch of white pepper
1 tbsp sugar

Mix the dark soy sauce, light soy sauce, 2 tablespoons of the yellow bean sauce and the Chinese rice wine together in a bowl and set to one side.

Place a saucepan that has a tight-fitting lid over a medium-low heat and add ½ tablespoon of the oil. Season the pork belly with a pinch of salt and white pepper, then add to the pan and cook for 6 minutes, turning frequently. Sprinkle in the sugar and continue to cook for a further 2 minutes. Pour in the soy sauce mixture and cook for another 1–2 minutes, then pour in 500ml (2 cups) water and mix well. Bring to a very gentle simmer, cover with the lid and cook slowly for 40 minutes. After 40 minutes, remove the lid and continue cooking until the sauce has almost gone. Remove the pan from the heat and set to one side.

Place a wok over a medium-high heat, add the remaining oil along with your noodles and cook for 2 minutes. Once the noodles have loosened and softened add the remaining 2 tablespoons of yellow bean sauce along with 3 tablespoons water and mix well. Once fully coated, transfer to serving bowls or plates. Cut the rested pork belly into slices and arrange over the noodles, drizzling with the leftover cooking sauce.

BEEF & OYSTER SAUCE WITH EGG NOODLES

Chinese chefs have been using oyster sauce to inject flavour into dishes of meat and vegetables for over 100 years, since its accidental creation in 1888. Making the most of its rich umami taste, this is my take on some of those classic Cantonese dishes.

10 MINUTES   **12 MINUTES**   **SERVES 4**

❶ 300g (10oz) straight-to-wok egg noodles

❷ 6 tbsp oyster sauce

❸ 340g (12oz) fillet of beef, cut into bite-sized pieces (see tip below)

❹ 2 garlic cloves, finely chopped or grated

❺ 1 head of broccoli, cut into bite-sized florets

From the store cupboard
3 tbsp vegetable oil
2 tbsp light soy sauce
1 tsp sugar
½ tsp salt
¼ tsp white pepper

Tip
Tenderising your beef in advance (page 12) will make a huge difference to the texture, though it's not essential.

Place a wok over a medium-high heat, add 1 tablespoon of the oil along with the noodles and cook for 2 minutes. Once the noodles have loosened and softened add 2 tablespoons of the oyster sauce along with 2 tablespoons water and mix well. Once the noodles are fully coated transfer to a serving plate and cover loosely with foil.

Quickly rinse your wok and wipe dry, then return to a medium-high heat and add another tablespoon of oil. Once the oil is smoking, add your beef and fry for 90 seconds to seal each piece (work in batches to avoid overcrowding the pan), then transfer to a plate and set to one side.

Add the final tablespoon of oil to the wok and fry the garlic for 90 seconds until fragrant, then add the broccoli and fry for a further minute. Add the remaining oyster sauce, the soy sauce, sugar, salt and pepper along with 120ml (½ cup) water, bringing it all to a gentle simmer, then turn the heat down to medium-low, cover and leave for 3 minutes. Finally add the cooked beef, mix well and serve over the noodles.

CANTON STEAK & ONIONS

This dish conjures up vivid childhood memories from the restaurant of a cast-iron bull-shaped skillet being heated until red hot over the range. It was then placed on a wooden board and the smell of scorched wood would fill the kitchen. Head Chef, Ben, would pour on tender pieces of fillet steak and sliced onion smothered in a rich, sweet, tangy sauce; as it hit the red-hot skillet the sauce would spit and sizzle and a billow of the most fragrant cloud would follow the waitress across the restaurant as she delivered the dish to the waiting guests.

5 MINUTES   **5 MINUTES**   **SERVES 2**

1 1 large Spanish onion, cut into strips

2 2 x 200–250g (7–9oz) fillet steaks, cut into bite-sized slices (see tip below)

3 5 tbsp Tonkatsu Sauce (page 134 or use shop-bought)

From the store cupboard
2 tbsp oil

Tip
Tenderising your beef in advance (page 12) will make a huge difference to the texture, though it's not essential.

Place a wok over a medium-high heat, add 2 tablespoons of the oil along with the sliced onion and stir-fry for 2 minutes.

Add the beef and sear on both sides; this will take about 2 minutes. Turn the heat down to medium and add the tonkatsu sauce along with 3 tablespoons water. Mix well and serve with either steamed or fried rice.

PORK ESCALOPE WITH TONKATSU SAUCE & STICKY RICE

Juicy pork is coated in the crispiest of crumbs, sliced into bite-sized pieces, layered over fragrant rice and smothered in a sweet, yet tangy sauce.

10 MINUTES **40 MINUTES** **SERVES 4**

❶ 360g (2 cups) glutinous rice (see tip below)

❷ 1 egg, beaten

❸ 50g (1 cup) panko breadcrumbs

❹ 340g (12oz) boneless pork chops, rind removed

❺ 120ml (½ cup) Tonkatsu Sauce (page 134 or use shop-bought)

From the store cupboard
500ml (2 cups) vegetable oil
½ tsp salt
¼ tsp white pepper

Tip
Glutinous rice is a medium- to long-grain variety of rice that becomes sticky once cooked. You can find glutinous rice at your local Chinese supermarket or from online suppliers.

Put the rice into a medium saucepan and fill with warm water. Wash the rice by rubbing it between your hands, then carefully drain. Repeat at least three times, as this process removes some of the starch. Drain the rice completely and return to the pan, then cover with exactly 500ml (2 cups) water. Turn the heat on to full and bring the rice to the boil – it is important you do not stir.

You must pay full attention to the pan now. Once the water has been absorbed and tiny craters appear in the rice, turn the heat down to its lowest setting and place a lid firmly on to the saucepan to seal in the steam. Don't be tempted to peek and remove the lid. Cook for a further 5 minutes and then turn off the heat completely. Leave to steam in the residual heat for a further 15 minutes. Remove the lid and stir the rice with a spoon to loosen the grains; it will feel very sticky.

Heat the oil in a deep saucepan to 170°C (340°F).

Put the beaten egg into a shallow bowl and season with salt and pepper. Put the breadcrumbs in another bowl. Dip each pork chop into the beaten egg, then coat in the panko breadcrumbs, pushing the chops down into the crumbs so that they stick and create a complete layer across the meat. Gently lower each chop into the heated oil and fry for 6–8 minutes, turning frequently to ensure even cooking and colour. Once you are happy that the pork is cooked through, drain on a wire rack or a plate lined with kitchen paper.

Once drained, slice the chops into bite-sized pieces and arrange over the sticky rice. Drizzle over the Tonkatsu Sauce and serve.

SWEET & SOUR PORK BALLS

What can I say about one of the most recognised Chinese takeaway dishes ever invented? These deep-fried balls – crispy on the outside, juicy in the middle – are oh so yummy. This recipe, or something similar, is pretty much used in every takeaway across the world.

10 MINUTES   **20 MINUTES**   **SERVES 4**

❶ 125g (1 cup) plain (all-purpose) flour

❷ 2 tsp baking powder

❸ 2 eggs

❹ 340g (12oz) boneless pork chops, rind removed and cut into 3cm (1¼in) cubes

❺ 120ml (½ cup) ready-made sweet and sour sauce

From the store cupboard
1 tsp salt
500ml (2 cups) vegetable oil

Tip
Keep any leftover batter in the fridge and use within 3 days.

In a large bowl mix together the flour, baking powder and salt.

In a separate bowl, beat together the eggs with 2 tablespoons of the oil and 250ml (1 cup) water. Add the wet mixture to the flour and mix well to create a smooth paste. Drop the pork into the flour paste, thoroughly coating each piece. You may have leftover batter (see tip below).

Preheat the remaining oil to 170°C (340°F) in a deep-sided wok or saucepan and carefully lower the coated pork into the oil one piece at a time, in batches of 8–10 pieces. Fry for 6–8 minutes until golden brown and cooked through. If you have a food probe thermometer, the internal temperature should reach 78°C (170°F). Remove the cooked pork from the oil and allow it to drain on a wire rack or a plate lined with kitchen paper.

If you like your sweet and sour balls super crispy, once they have cooled for 10 minutes, simply drop them back in the oil for a second fry for a couple of minutes.

Warm your sweet and sour sauce, arrange the crispy pork balls on a plate and serve with the sauce.

BLACK PEPPER BEEF

There's something quite special about fillet steak coated in a rich black pepper sauce and cooked with strips of onion and green peppers. The meat literally soaks up all of the flavours.

 10 MINUTES   **10 MINUTES**   **SERVES 4**

1 1 tbsp whole black peppercorns

2 340g (12oz) beef fillet, sliced (see tip below)

3 1 Spanish onion, cut into strips

4 1 green (bell) pepper, cut into strips

5 2 tbsp oyster sauce

From the store cupboard
2 tbsp oil
2 tbsp light soy sauce
1 tsp sugar
½ tsp salt

Tip
Tenderising your beef in advance (page 12) will make a huge difference to the texture, though it's not essential.

Coarsely grind the peppercorns in a pestle and mortar – not too fine, but you also don't want to be crunching down on any whole peppercorns either.

Place a wok over a medium-high heat and add 1 tablespoon of the oil; once smoking, add the beef and fry for 90 seconds to seal each piece. Transfer to a plate and set to one side.

Add the remaining oil to the wok and fry the onion and pepper strips for 2 minutes. Once the onion is translucent, add the oyster sauce, soy sauce, sugar and salt along with 3 tablespoons water. Bring to the boil, then reduce the heat and simmer for 3 minutes, or until the sauce has thickened. Stir in the cooked beef and serve immediately.

VEGETARIAN

BAKED MUSHROOMS WITH A FIVE-SPICE CRUST

Served with noodles, rice, salad or even in a freshly steamed bao, these juicy and aromatic mushrooms with a crispy crumb pretty much work with everything.

5 MINUTES   **20 MINUTES**   **SERVES 2-4**

1 4 large mushrooms (flat or portobello)

2 1 onion, finely diced

3 50g (1 cup) fresh breadcrumbs

4 1 tbsp Chinese five spice

5 1 tbsp garlic powder

From the store cupboard
2 tbsp oil (vegetable, groundnut or coconut)
1 tbsp salt
½ tsp white pepper

Clean the mushrooms and remove the stalks. Gently rub in a little of the oil and sprinkle with a little of the salt and pepper and set to one side.

Heat a large non-stick wok or frying pan over a medium-high heat, add 1 tablespoon of oil and fry the onion for 2 minutes. Add the breadcrumbs, Chinese five spice, garlic powder and the remaining salt and pepper and continue to fry for a further 2 minutes, making sure the ingredients are well mixed. Remove from the heat.

Preheat the oven to 200°C (400°F).

Using a spoon, fill each of the mushrooms with the breadcrumb mixture. Place filled-side up on a baking tray and bake in the oven for 20 minutes. Remove from the oven and serve.

CHILLI GINGER
CRISPY TOFU

For those of you who love sweet, spicy and crispy in a single mouthful, this dish will have your taste buds singing. The crispy fried tofu drinks up all of that lovely tangy sweet and spicy sauce as it is tossed through the wok.

5 MINUTES   **15 MINUTES**   **SERVES 2**

1 340g (12oz) firm tofu, cut into bite-sized pieces

2 2 tbsp grated fresh ginger

3 4 garlic cloves, finely chopped or grated

4 3 tbsp dried chilli flakes

5 4 tbsp rice vinegar

From the store cupboard
300ml (1¼ cups) vegetable oil, plus 1 tbsp
3 tbsp light soy sauce
2 tbsp sugar

Preheat the 300ml (1¼ cups) oil in a saucepan to 175°C (350°F) and carefully lower in the tofu pieces. Fry for 6–8 minutes until golden brown. Drain on kitchen paper and set to one side.

Place a wok over a medium heat, add the 1 tablespoon of oil and gently fry the ginger and garlic until fragrant, taking care not to burn. After 1 minute, add the chilli flakes and fry for a further minute. Add the soy sauce, rice vinegar and sugar and continue to cook until the sauce has thickened. Toss in the cooked tofu, turn to coat evenly and serve.

AUBERGINE FRITTERS WITH HOISIN DIP

My juicy and crispy aubergine fritters make a perfect late-night snack. Curl up on the sofa, pop on your favourite film and scoff away; sounds like heaven to me!

 5 MINUTES   **10 MINUTES**   **SERVES 2-4**

1 180g (1½ cups) plain (all-purpose) flour

2 ¼ tsp baking powder

3 600ml (2½ cups) sparkling water

4 1 large aubergine (eggplant), cut into 5mm (¼in) slices

5 4 tbsp hoisin sauce

From the store cupboard
500ml (2 cups) vegetable oil
½ tsp salt

Pour the oil into a large saucepan and heat to 175°C (350°F).

In a large bowl, combine the flour, baking powder and salt. Add the sparkling water and use a fork to mix together. It is perfectly fine to have small lumps of flour in your mixture; it's more important not to overwork the mixture as this will build up the gluten in the flour and make your batter doughy.

One slice at a time, dip the aubergine into the batter and then carefully lower into the oil. Fry in small batches for 3–5 minutes, turning occasionally for even cooking and colour. Drain on kitchen paper and serve hot with hoisin sauce for dipping.

ROASTED TOFU SALAD

How do you pimp up your salad bowl? I like to add spicy aromatic satay tofu pieces and toss these in a big bowl of salad leaves with crunchy, creamy cashew nuts and zingy ringlets of spring onion.

10 MINUTES

25 MINUTES

SERVES 2

1 3 tbsp salted cashew nuts, crushed into small pieces

2 2 tbsp satay sauce

3 340g (12oz) firm tofu, cut into bite-sized pieces

4 1 bag of mixed salad leaves

5 3 spring onions (scallions), cut into rings

From the store cupboard
3 tbsp light soy sauce
2 tbsp vegetable oil
1 tbsp sugar

Preheat the oven to 180°C (350°F).

In a large bowl, combine 1 tablespoon of the crushed cashew nuts with the satay sauce, soy sauce, vegetable oil and sugar. Gently fold in the tofu pieces so each is coated with marinade (you may need to loosen the sauce with a tablespoon of water if it's too thick).

Arrange the tofu pieces in a single layer on a baking sheet and bake in the oven for 20–25 minutes. Remove from the oven and allow to cool.

Arrange the salad leaves on a serving plate, sprinkle over the cooked tofu and gently toss before adding a final garnish of crushed cashew nuts and chopped spring onions.

SEARED AUBERGINE WITH MISO & SESAME SEEDS

Aubergines have the ability to absorb all the flavours from their surrounding ingredients, so when you add garlic, the rich intense umami flavour of miso paste and nutty toasted sesame seeds, you know you're on to a winner.

10 MINUTES   **12 MINUTES**   **SERVES 2**

1 2 tbsp sesame seeds

2 2 garlic cloves, finely chopped or grated

3 2 large aubergines (eggplants), cut into bite-sized pieces

4 2 tbsp red miso paste

5 2 tbsp rice wine

From the store cupboard
2 tbsp oil
1 tsp sugar
½ tsp salt
¼ tsp white pepper
2 tbsp light soy sauce

Place a non-stick pan over a medium-high heat, wipe completely dry with kitchen paper and then add the sesame seeds and toast until lightly browned and fragrant. Transfer to a bowl and set to one side.

Place a wok over a medium heat, add the oil and gently fry the garlic until fragrant. Add the aubergine and fry for a further minute, then add 4 tablespoons water, turn down to a simmer and cover with a lid. Cook for 6–8 minutes.

Once the aubergine has softened, remove the lid. Add the miso paste, rice wine, sugar, salt, pepper and soy sauce, combine well and continue cooking until the liquid has reduced by half.

Transfer to a serving plate, sprinkle over the toasted sesame seeds and enjoy.

CHILLI BEAN TOFU & VEGETABLE SKEWERS

What is it about eating food with your hands? It must be a primal thing but somehow I find that it always tastes better. These tofu vegetable skewers are one such dish that I especially enjoy eating with my hands.

10 MINUTES   **10 MINUTES**   **SERVES 4**

1 2 tbsp chilli bean sauce

2 1 tbsp tomato purée (paste)

3 340g (12oz) firm tofu, cut into 3cm (1¼in) cubes

4 6 fresh baby corn, cut in half

5 1 red (bell) pepper, cut into bite-sized cubes

From the store cupboard
1 tbsp sugar
2 tbsp soy sauce
2 tbsp vegetable oil

Tip
These are great cooked on a barbecue, as the smoky flavour really adds to the already tasty skewers.

If using wooden skewers, it's a good idea to soak them in warm water for about 10 minutes before cooking to stop them from burning.

Combine the chilli bean sauce, tomato purée, sugar and soy sauce in a bowl.

Preheat your grill (broiler) to medium-high. Thread the tofu, baby corn and red pepper cubes on to the skewers and brush with the chilli bean sauce. I'd recommend 2 skewers per person. Lay on a baking tray and place under the grill for 8–10 minutes, turning frequently and brushing with more sauce (this will build up a tasty layer).

Once browned all over, tender and covered in sauce, transfer to a serving plate.

SRIRACHA LO MEIN

Lo mein is cooked ever so slightly differently to chow mein; chow mein is stir-fried until the noodles are crispy whereas lo mein is stir-fried with a sauce so that they remain soft. Sriracha is a delicious sauce originating from Thailand and works well with vegetables and noodles.

10 MINUTES   **8 MINUTES**   **SERVES 2**

① 3 tbsp Sriracha chilli sauce

② 2 nests of fresh lo mein egg noodles

③ 1 red (bell) pepper, cut into strips

④ 8 fresh baby corn, halved lengthways

⑤ 175g (3½ cups) beansprouts

From the store cupboard
2 tbsp soy sauce
1 tsp sugar
2 tbsp vegetable oil
pinch of salt

Combine the Sriracha sauce, soy sauce and sugar in a bowl and set to one side

Loosen the noodles in a bowl of warm water, then drain and set to one side.

Place a wok over a medium-high heat, add the oil and fry the red pepper and baby corn for 1 minute. Add the beansprouts and fry for a further minute, then add the loosened noodles along with the sauce mix and continue to fry until all of the ingredients are combined and warmed through. Serve immediately.

BLACK BEAN TOFU AND VEGETABLE STIR-FRY

Tofu has been used in China for well over 2,000 years. As a staple ingredient for vegetarian Buddhist monks, Buddhist chefs often shape and cook the tofu to resemble meat. Black bean fried tofu can be found on many Cantonese restaurant menus and is still one of the top ordered vegetarian dishes.

 5 MINUTES   **8 MINUTES**   **SERVES 2**

1 4 tbsp fermented Chinese black beans

2 340g (12oz) firm tofu, cut into bite-sized pieces

3 2 garlic cloves, finely chopped or grated

4 1 bag of ready-prepared stir-fry vegetables

5 1 tbsp cornflour (cornstarch) mixed with 2 tbsp water

From the store cupboard
2 tbsp vegetable oil
½ tsp salt
¼ tsp white pepper
1 tsp sugar
2 tbsp light soy sauce

Soak the fermented black beans in 120ml (½ cup) water for 10 minutes, then drain in a sieve and set to one side.

Heat the oil in a wok over a medium-high heat and fry the tofu for 6–8 minutes until golden brown on all sides. Drain on kitchen paper and set to one side.

Reheat the oiled wok over a medium heat and gently fry the garlic and black beans for 45 seconds until fragrant. Add the stir-fry vegetables, increase the heat to medium-high and fry for 2 minutes. Then add 120ml (½ cup) water, the salt, pepper, sugar, soy sauce and fried tofu and bring to the boil.

Give the cornflour mixture a stir and slowly pour into the sauce, stirring constantly, to thicken. Serve immediately.

MUSHROOM CURRY

During the time of the old Silk Road, when traders from China were transporting their silks into Europe, they would pick up new ingredients and cooking methods along the way. So was the Chinese curry developed in this way? There are many theories; all I know is I love Chinese curry!

5 MINUTES   **10 MINUTES**   **SERVES 2**

1 4 squares of Chinese or Japanese curry sauce mix (bought in a block)

2 1 Spanish onion, cut into cubes

3 340g (12oz) closed-cup mushrooms, cut into bite-sized pieces

4 30g (¼ cup) frozen peas

From the store cupboard
1 tbsp vegetable oil
pinch of salt
pinch of white pepper
pinch of sugar

Make up your curry sauce following the instructions on the packet.

Place your wok over a medium-high heat, add the oil and fry the onion for 2 minutes until translucent. Add the mushrooms along with the salt, pepper and sugar. Once the mushrooms have softened, stir in the peas and the prepared curry sauce and simmer for 3 minutes, then serve.

BOILED RICE

This is how I was taught to cook boiled rice; it's known as the absorption method and in my 40-plus years of cooking this method has never let me down. However, every now and then I get distracted and I forget to turn the rice down once the water has evaporated, leaving me with a burnt saucepan and charred smell that lingers for days, but that's purely my own fault for being so easily distr— 'Squirrel!'

5 MINUTES   **25 MINUTES**   **SERVES 4**

1 360g (2 cups) Thai fragrant rice

Put the rice into a medium saucepan and fill with warm water. Wash the rice by rubbing it between your hands, then carefully drain. Repeat at least three times, as this process removes some of the starch. Drain the rice completely and return to the pan, then cover with 2.5cm (1in) water. Turn the heat on to full and bring the rice to the boil – it is important you do not stir.

You must pay full attention to the pan now. Once the water has been absorbed and tiny craters appear in the rice, turn the heat down to its lowest setting and place a lid firmly on to the saucepan to seal in the steam. Don't be tempted to peek and remove the lid. Cook for a further 5 minutes and then turn off the heat completely. Leave to steam in the residual heat for a further 15 minutes. Remove the lid and stir the rice with a spoon to loosen the grains.

CONDIMENTS

WASABI MAYO

For those of you who haven't made your own mayonnaise before, you won't believe just how simple it is until you've gone ahead and done it. And for those of you who love the idea of a wasabi mayo but don't have the inclination to make your own from scratch, simply mix the wasabi into shop-bought mayonnaise. To make a Sriracha mayo, simply replace the wasabi with the same amount of Sriracha.

5 MINUTES   **SERVES 8–10**

❶ 3 egg yolks

❷ 300ml (1¼ cups) groundnut oil

❸ 2 tbsp wasabi paste

❹ 1 tbsp lemon juice

❺ pinch of black pepper

From the store cupboard
pinch of salt

Tip
If you don't have a food processor, you can use a large bowl and a balloon whisk. Place a folded tea towel on your work surface and put the bowl on top to stop it from slipping around during mixing. Add the egg yolks and begin to whisk and as you whisk, very slowly drizzle in the oil, a few drops at a time. Once half of the oil has been added, you can begin to add the oil a little quicker, and when all of the oil has been added you can add the flavourings and whisk again for 5–10 seconds.

Put your egg yolks into a food processor and begin to blend on medium speed, then very slowly drizzle the oil into the mixture. Once half of the oil has been added you can begin to add the oil a little quicker, and when all of the oil has been added and thoroughly mixed in, turn off the blender. Add the wasabi paste, lemon juice, salt and black pepper and blend again for 5–10 seconds.

HOT CHILLI DRAGON SAUCE

The aroma from this sauce fills your kitchen like no other; it's aromatic, it's spicy, it's quite simply amazing. I love the sound of the sizzle as you pour the oil into the soy sauce. You won't have tasted anything quite like this dip before, but you will want to use it again and again once you have.

5 MINUTES   **5 MINUTES**   **SERVES 4**

1 3–5 green bird's-eye chillies, finely chopped

2 3 spring onions (scallions), thinly sliced into ringlets

From the store cupboard
4 tbsp soy sauce
4 tbsp vegetable oil

Put the chopped chillies and spring onions into a heatproof bowl, pour over the soy sauce and mix well.

Heat the oil in a saucepan until it begins to smoke a little, then remove from heat and slowly and carefully drizzle over the soy sauce mixture. It will sizzle and spit (like a dragon) and it will fill the air with an amazing aroma.

This dip is great with everything.

TONKATSU SAUCE

This tangy, sweet, aromatic sauce is normally served with deep-fried cutlets but it really does work with anything. Not too dissimilar to a good barbecue sauce, you can dip a myriad of goodies into this sticky, unctuous condiment.

5 MINUTES   **SERVES 4**

① 1¼ tsp garlic powder

② 600ml (2½ cups) tomato ketchup

③ 12 tbsp Worcestershire sauce

From the store cupboard
5 tbsp light soy sauce
8 tbsp sugar

Put all of the ingredients into a small saucepan and gently warm. Once the sugar has completely dissolved, remove from the heat. Be careful not to boil.

Once completely cooled, transfer to an airtight container and store in the fridge for up to 2 weeks. You can also freeze in ice-cube trays for up to 3 months.

CHINESE BARBECUE SAUCE

The epitome of all Chinese sauces and one that many, if not all of us, know and love across the world. This sauce works really well as a marinade; I also enjoy it as a dipping sauce.

15 MINUTES   **SERVES 8**

1 1 x 400g (14oz) can hoisin barbecue sauce

2 1 x 400g (14oz) can yellow bean sauce

3 1½ tbsp Chinese five spice

4 4 tbsp Chinese rice wine

5 1.5 litres (6 cups) vegetable stock

From the store cupboard
5 tbsp white sugar

Put all of the ingredients into a saucepan and slowly bring to a simmer. Simmer for 15 minutes and then remove from heat.

Once fully cooled, pour the sauce into an airtight container and store in the fridge for up to a week, or pour into individual ice-cube trays and freeze. Once frozen, place the cubes into a ziplock bag and store in the freezer for up to 6 months. Allow 2–3 cubes per portion, which can be reheated from frozen.

STIR-FRY SAUCE

Having a pre-made stir-fry sauce is a godsend to the home cook who is fighting time or is simply too tired to pull out half the cupboard to cook a meal. Made by combining classic Chinese flavours, it can be added to noodles, rice, meat and vegetables to quickly and easily vamp up your meal.

5 MINUTES   **SERVES 12–16**

1 12 tbsp oyster sauce
2 5 tbsp light soy sauce
3 3 tbsp dark soy sauce
4 3 tbsp sesame oil
5 3 tbsp Shaoxing wine

Combine all of the ingredients in a large bowl and mix well.

Store in an airtight jar in the fridge for up to 1 month or pour into an ice-cube tray and freeze for up to 3 months.

SWEET PICKLED CUCUMBER

Pickling has been used for thousands of years as a practical method of preserving food. I've found that nowadays, pickles are used to refresh the palate, especially if eating rich or very sweet dishes. These pickled cucumbers are a tasty accompaniment served on the side of your plate or even eaten as a snack.

2 HOURS 5 MINUTES   **3 MINUTES**   **SERVES 4**

1 250ml (1 cup) rice vinegar

2 1 cucumber, deseeded and cut into batons or half-moons

From the store cupboard
75g (⅓ cup) sugar
1½ tsp salt

In a saucepan over a medium-low heat, gently dissolve the sugar and salt in the rice vinegar. Once dissolved, remove from the heat and set to one side to cool.

In a large container (preferably glass), add the cucumber pieces and pour over the cooled vinegar liquid, making sure as much of the cucumber as possible is submerged. Cover and place in the fridge, removing after 1 hour to give the cucumber a good mix. Re-cover and place back in the fridge, leaving to pickle for at least 2 hours before eating, but ideally leave overnight.

This will keep for up to a month in an airtight container in the fridge.

FIVE SPICE WEDGES

Who doesn't love wedges? I just had to include a recipe for my take on this favourite side dish. Seasoned with Chinese flavours and cooked in a crispy coating, I hope that you love them as much as I do.

15 MINUTES   **45 MINUTES**   **SERVES 2**

❶ 3 large floury potatoes, scrubbed but left unpeeled

❷ 150g (1 cup) dried polenta (cornmeal)

❸ ½ tbsp garlic salt

❹ ½ tbsp paprika

❺ 1 tsp Chinese five spice

From the store cupboard
4 tbsp vegetable oil

Cut the potatoes into wedges of roughly the same size and add to a large saucepan of water. Place over a medium-high heat, bring to the boil and cook for 5–6 minutes until tender. Drain and allow to cool.

Put the cooled wedges into a large bowl with the oil and gently turn to coat evenly. Tip the dried polenta on to a large plate and toss the oiled wedges in it to coat evenly, gently tapping off any excess.

Preheat the oven to 180°C (350°F) and spread the potato wedges on a baking tray in a single layer and bake for 30 minutes.

Mix together the remaining ingredients and set to one side.

After 30 minutes, sprinkle the wedges with some of the seasoning mix and return to the oven to bake for a further 10–15 minutes. Remove from the oven, tip into a large, clean bowl and sprinkle with the remaining seasoning, tossing gently to evenly coat the wedges. Serve immediately.

LUCKY SEVEN SEASONING SALT

After I opened my Hong Kong-style noodle bar, Wantons, a few years ago, I began designing a spice mix that could be added to wings, ribs and – of course – fries. After a few attempts, this is what I came up with and the customers seemed to really enjoy it. Sprinkle over your fried goodies for a taste explosion.

5 MINUTES   **SERVES 20+**

1 1 tbsp paprika
2 1 tbsp Chinese five spice
3 2 tbsp garlic powder
4 2 tbsp onion powder
5 3 tbsp celery salt

From the store cupboard
70g (¼ cup) salt
½ tbsp white pepper

Combine all of the ingredients in a large bowl and then transfer to a bone dry airtight container. This will happily sit on your shelf for 3 months.

DESSERTS & DRINKS

LYCHEE & MANGO PUDDING

My version of an Eton mess without the meringue: sweet, juicy lychee and mango smothered in a sweet, thick cream and flecked with black peppercorns – a little play on that sweet and savoury that we all love.

10 MINUTES   **SERVES 4**

1 12 lychees (fresh or canned)

2 1 mango (fresh or canned), peeled, stoned and cut into bite-sized pieces

3 300ml (1¼ cups) double (heavy) cream

4 1½ tbsp icing (confectioners') sugar

5 ½ tsp crushed black peppercorns

From the store cupboard
pinch of salt

If you are using fresh lychees, peel them and remove their stones but try to keep them whole. If you are using canned lychees or mango, drain, chop and set to one side.

Whisk the double cream in a large bowl until it has thickened to the same consistency as a thick custard. Sift in the sugar and salt, then add the crushed black peppercorns, lychees and mango and carefully fold through until completely combined. Portion into serving bowls and dive in.

KWOKLYN'S CHILLI ICE CREAM

If you have never tried chilli ice cream, you are missing out! It is creamy, smooth and cool at first and then slowly you begin to feel the warm heat building in your mouth. As the heat develops you realise you need to have another mouthful to cool things down; and so the cycle begins again!

5 MINUTES   **30 MINUTES**   **SERVES 6**

1 5 Thai red chillies, deseeded and very finely chopped

2 600ml (2½ cups) double (heavy) cream

3 1 x 397g (14oz) can condensed milk

4 1 tsp cornflour (cornstarch)

5 3 drops of chilli extract (optional)

From the store cupboard
2 tbsp sugar

Place a non-stick wok over a medium heat, add the finely chopped chilli and dry fry gently for 2–3 minutes, then add 80ml (⅓ cup) water and gently simmer for another 2–3 minutes, allowing the chillies to soften. Add the sugar, combine and continue to cook until you have a syrupy chilli mix. Turn off the heat and allow it to cool for 15 minutes.

Pour the double cream into a large bowl and whisk until you have stiff peaks, then add the condensed milk, cornflour, cooled chilli syrup and chilli extract (if using) and continue to whisk until the mixture has thickened.

Transfer to an airtight container and freeze for at least 8 hours.

BANANA FRITTERS

A classic Chinese restaurant dessert. This delicious choice was one of the customer favourites when I was growing up.

10 MINUTES   **15 MINUTES**   **SERVES 4**

❶ 250g (2 cups) self-raising flour, plus extra for dusting

❷ ½ tsp bicarbonate of soda (baking soda)

❸ 4 bananas, peeled and halved

❹ 6 tbsp golden (light corn) syrup

❺ 4 scoops of vanilla ice cream

From the store cupboard
vegetable oil for deep-frying

Heat the vegetable oil in a large, deep saucepan to 170°C (340°F). Fill the pan about two-thirds full.

Sift the self-raising flour into a large bowl and add the bicarbonate of soda. Pour in 375ml (1½ cups) water, mixing until you have a smooth batter.

Lightly dust the bananas in a little extra flour and dip into the batter. Working in batches of 2, carefully lower the bananas into the hot oil and fry for 6–8 minutes until golden brown, turning frequently as they cook. Once browned and lightly floating, place on a wire rack or a plate lined with kitchen paper to drain.

Transfer to a serving plate and drizzle over the golden syrup. Serve with a scoop of vanilla ice cream.

NUTELLA MOCHI

Mochi is made by pounding glutinous rice flour to make a sticky, chewy dough. It is then filled with a variety of fillings and eaten as a sweet snack. This is my take on the sweet treat and I hope you agree that it's nothing short of yummy.

15 MINUTES   **15 MINUTES**   **SERVES 4**

1 160g (1 cup) glutinous rice flour (see tip below)

2 cornflour (cornstarch), for dusting

3 3 tbsp Nutella

4 3 tbsp crunchy peanut butter

5 35g (¼ cup) toasted sesame seeds

From the store cupboard
400g (2 cups) sugar

Tip
Glutinous rice flour is made from sweet white rice that becomes moist and sticky once cooked. You can find glutinous rice flour at your local Chinese supermarket or from online suppliers.

You can add any filling you like to mochi, such as red bean paste, black sesame paste, lotus seed paste or even your favourite jam, marmalade or a dollop of frozen ice cream.

Put the rice flour, 180ml (¾ cup) cold water and the sugar into a large microwavable bowl and mix to combine. Cover the bowl with cling film (plastic wrap) and place it into the microwave for 3 minutes on full power. Remove from the microwave and vigorously mix for 3 minutes, then re-cover with cling film and return to the microwave for a further 3 minutes on full power. Vigorously mix again for a further 3 minutes.

Dust your work surface generously with cornflour, turn out the mixture and begin to knead vigorously for up to 10 minutes. The mixture should feel very springy and be medium firm. Separate the dough into 12 equal pieces and roll into balls.

Take one ball and flatten into a disc about 7cm (2¾in) in diameter. Put 1 teaspoon of Nutella and 1 teaspoon of peanut butter into the centre of the disc, then fold in the edges to cover the filling and reshape into a smooth ball. Roll the ball into the toasted sesame seeds to evenly cover and set to one side while you finish the rest.

Once all of the mochi have been made they are ready to serve.

CHINESE TOFFEE APPLES

In my experience, every Chinese restaurant serves this dish and here's why: juicy sweet apples are coated in a crisp doughnut batter then smothered in molten sugar and toasted sesame seeds. It's no wonder really that this dish is a firm favourite.

10 MINUTES　　**15 MINUTES**　　**SERVES 4**

1 250g (2 cups) self-raising flour, plus extra for dusting

2 1 egg, beaten

3 4–6 apples, peeled and chopped into 3cm (1¼in) cubes

4 2 tbsp sesame seeds

From the store cupboard
vegetable oil for deep-frying, plus 1 tbsp for frying
10 tbsp sugar

Pour the vegetable oil for deep-frying into a large, deep saucepan and heat to 170°C (340°F). Fill the pan about two-thirds full.

Sift the self-raising flour into a large bowl, then add the beaten egg along with 375ml (1½ cups) water and mix until you have a smooth batter.

Lightly dust the apples in a little extra flour and dip into the batter, then carefully lower into the oil. Fry for 6–8 minutes until golden brown, turning frequently during cooking. Once browned and floating, place on a wire rack or a plate lined with kitchen paper to drain.

Heat the 1 tablespoon of oil in a wok over a medium heat and stir in the sugar. After about 3 minutes the sugar should begin to caramelise; at this point gently add the apples and the sesame seeds. Mix well, being really careful not to splash the molten sugar or break up the apple casings but making sure each apple piece is thoroughly covered. Turn off the heat.

Using a pair of tongs or chopsticks, drop each piece of apple into a large bowl of ice-cold water, this will instantly harden your toffee apple bites and help them keep their round shape. As soon as the toffee has hardened transfer to a wire rack or kitchen paper to drain. Serve and enjoy.

CHINESE FRIED SESAME BALLS

As a child I always remember Dad ordering these when we first arrived at a restaurant to eat. I've found that many Chinese people tend to have fruit at the end of a meal, so sweet treats like these are eaten at the beginning and could be enjoyed as a little appetizer.

15 MINUTES   **15 MINUTES**   **SERVES 8**

1 110g (½ cup) soft light brown sugar

2 250g (1½ cups) glutinous rice flour, plus extra for dusting (see tip below)

3 6 tbsp sweet lotus seed paste (or use red bean paste or Nutella)

4 70g (½ cup) sesame seeds

From the store cupboard
vegetable oil for deep-frying

Tip
Glutinous rice flour is made from sweet white rice that becomes moist and sticky once cooked. You can find glutinous rice flour at your local Chinese supermarket or from online suppliers.

In a large jug, mix the brown sugar with 160ml (²/₃ cup) hot water, stirring until completely dissolved.

Put the rice flour into a large bowl and create a well in the middle. Add the sugar water and mix into the flour; continue to mix for 5 minutes until the dough stops sticking to the bowl.

Lightly dust your work surface with rice flour, turn out the dough and knead for 5 minutes until the dough becomes smooth. You can use a little more flour or water to achieve this if required.

Divide the dough into 8 equal pieces, roll into small balls and then flatten into discs about 7cm (2¾in) in diameter. Place 2 teaspoons of your chosen paste into the centre of each disc, then fold in the edges to cover the filling and reshape into smooth balls. Roll the balls in the sesame seeds to evenly cover.

Heat the oil in a large, deep saucepan to about 165°C (330°F) – you don't want to fry the balls at too high a temperature. Fill the pan about two-thirds full. Working in batches of 4, gently lower the balls into the oil and fry for 15 minutes. During this time you will need to frequently turn them so they achieve an even golden brown all over. As the balls cook they will expand and begin to float, so ensure there is plenty of room in the pan and cook in smaller batches if it works better with the pan you are using. Transfer to a wire rack or plate lined with kitchen paper to drain. Allow to cool for 20 minutes before serving.

LYCHEE CRUSH

This drink will have you romanticising about sandy beaches, hot summer afternoons and the gentle wash of the sea lapping across the shore. Sweet, juicy and creamy, it's a drink that slips down so smoothly, kicking your taste buds into action on the way through.

2 MINUTES　　**SERVES 4**

① 650ml (2¾ cups) lychee juice

② 6 tbsp condensed milk (you can use a vegan alternative)

③ 300ml (1¼ cups) coconut milk

④ 3 cups crushed ice

⑤ 1 x 420g (15oz) can lychees

Put all of the ingredients into a blender, reserving 4 whole lychees for decoration. Blend on full power for 20–30 seconds.

Pour into four glasses and top each one with a whole lychee.

HONG KONG-STYLE BUBBLE TEA

Bubble tea is a sweet tea-based drink that is served with chewy tapioca pearls, creating a drink and a meal all in one. It's a fun drink and quite unique. I used to serve this delicious recipe in my bubble tea bar in Leicester.

15 MINUTES   **3 MINUTES**   **SERVES 4**

1 150g (1 cup) tapioca pearls

2 5 tea bags

3 1 x 397g (14oz) can condensed milk

4 500ml (2 cups) strong black coffee

5 ice

Cook the tapioca pearls according to the packet instructions. Once fully cooked and softened, drain and set to one side.

Bring 1 litre (4 cups) water to the boil in a saucepan, add the tea bags and simmer for 2 minutes. Remove from the heat, discard the teabags and add the condensed milk, stirring until completely dissolved, then stir in the coffee. Fill a jug with as much ice as you can and pour the coffee/tea into the jug.

Spoon 3 tablespoons of cooked tapioca pearls into each of 4 glasses and add a couple of ice cubes. Fill with your chilled coffee/tea.

INDEX

ACKNOWLEDGEMENTS

From my parents that moulded me to be the person I am today, to the friends and supporters that helped to drive me forwards in my food inspired adventures; I thank you all, as none of this would have been possible without you.

Huge appreciation as always goes to the amazing team at Quadrille, Hardie Grant and my fantastic publishing agent Clare Hulton; you all shared my vision and thanks to you, the rest of the world can now share my recipes!

Kwoklyn

Kwoklyn Wan is a chef and broadcaster. He learnt the tools of his trade working in his family's Cantonese restaurant in Leicester. Kwoklyn now teaches and demos Chinese cooking, and is a martial arts instructor.